Ties That Bind

Ties That Bind

The Interdependence Of Generations

Eric R. Kingson
Barbara A. Hirshorn
John M. Cornman

A report from the Gerontological Society of America

Seven Locks Press

Publishers
Washington, D.C. / Cabin John, Md.

Note: The Gerontological Society of America (GSA) is a national multi-disciplinary professional membership organization dedicated to promoting the scientific study of aging, to fostering the expansion and dissemination of knowledge relating to gerontology, and to providing a forum for researchers and practitioners. The nonprofit Society's worldwide membership of 5700 represents clinical medicine, biology, and the behavioral and social sciences. Headquartered in Washington, GSA convenes annual scientific meetings, confers major awards, and publishes two journals, a newsletter, books, and monographs. Its mailing address is 1411 K Street, N.W., Suite 300, Washington, D. C. 20005.

Library of Congress Cataloging in Publication Data

Kingson, Eric R.
  Ties that bind

    "A report from the Gerontological Society of America."
    Includes index
    1. Aged—United States—Social conditions.
  2. Aged—Government policy—United States. 3. Intergenerational relations—
  United States. 4. Social security—United States.
  I. Hirshorn, Barbara A., 1948-   . II. Cornman, John M., 1933-
  III. Gerontological Society of America. IV. Title.
  HQ1064.U5K477 1986   305.2'6'0973   86-17664
  ISBN 0-932020-44-5 (pbk.)

Manufactured in the United States of America

Designed by Dan Thomas

Printed by the Maple Press Company, York, Pennsylvania

First edition, October 1986

Credits

1. Photos on front and back cover by Claire Flanders, Washington.

2 . Charts and tables appearing on pages 38, 40-45, 47, and 48 reprinted with permission from the Senate Special Committee on Aging, in conjunction with the American Association of Retired Persons, the Federal Council on Aging, and the Administration on Aging, *Aging in America: Trends and Projections, 1985-86* (Washington, D.C.: U.S. GPO, 1985).

Seven Locks Press

Publishers
P. O. Box 27
Cabin John, Maryland 20818
202-362-4714

Foreword

AMERICA is aging, and the projected magnitude of changes in the population is clear. The number of people aged 65 and over is expected to increase from 29 million to 65 million by 2030. By the same year, the number of persons 85 and over will have grown from 2.7 million to 8.6 million. One study projects the number of elderly needing some kind of long-term care jumping from 6.6 million in 1985 to 12.9 million in 2020.

It is also clear that changes of these magnitudes will require new responses from the public and private sectors. Far less clear are the desired shape and, in some instances, even the desired goals of the responses. In fact, the nature of the nation's response to an aging society is very much part of the current debate over federal budgets and deficits and the future role of government in the United States, a debate complicated by concerns for the growing rate of poverty among the nation's children, uncertainties about the impacts of the federal debt on the economic future of the country, and sharp differences on federal spending for domestic and defense programs.

Planning an effective response to the implications of an aging society is further complicated by lack of consensus for a policy framework within which to assess policy options. Perhaps the lack of such consensus is not surprising. Given the fact that an aging population is a new phenomenon, the nation has little experience on which to draw for guidance.

It is important, however, to understand not only that such a consensus is lacking, but that the policy framework finally agreed on will shape the questions society asks about and the responses society gives to the challenges posed by an aging population. This report, then, is not concerned with particular policy prescriptions, but with the broader and more basic issue of how our society ought to approach the challenges of this unprecedented prospect.

To oversimplify the choice of approaches, the aging of our population can be viewed as a success or a burden. Obviously, these disparate views would lead to sharply contrasting conclusions and policy recommendations.

This report seeks to clarify the search for an appropriate policy framework by providing information about the makeup of our older population and by pointing out issues and questions critical to determining the appropriateness of proposed frameworks. We hope the report generates the quality and quantity of public discussion the search deserves.

The Project Steering Committee

Marjorie H. Cantor, M.A. (Chair)
Brookdale Professor of Gerontology
  and Associate Director
Third Age Center
Fordham University
New York, New York

Richard C. Adelman, Ph.D.
Director
Institute of Gerontology
University of Michigan
Ann Arbor, Michigan

Harold Johnson, M.S.W.
Dean
School of Social Work
University of Michigan
Ann Arbor, Michigan

Robert L. Kane, M.D.
Dean
School of Public Health
University of Minnesota
Minneapolis, Minnesota

M. Powell Lawton, Ph.D.
Director of Behavioral Research
Philadelphia Geriatric Center
Philadelphia, Pennsylvania

James H. Schulz, Ph.D.
Professor of Welfare Economics
Florence Heller Graduate School
Brandeis University
Waltham, Massachusetts

Beth Soldo, Ph.D.
Associate Professor
Center for Population Research
Georgetown University
Washington, D.C.

The National Advisory Committee

Monsignor Charles J. Fahey (Chair)
Director
Third Age Center
Fordham University
New York, New York

Robert M. Ball
Visiting Scholar
Center for the Study of Social Policy
Washington, D.C.

Louise D. Crooks
National Vice President
American Association of Retired
  Persons
Washington, D.C.

James R. Dumpson, Ph.D.
Vice President
The New York Community Trust
New York, New York

Ina Guzman
Program Officer
John A. Hartford Foundation
New York, New York

Senator John Heinz
Chairman
Special Committee on Aging
U.S. Senate
Washington, D.C.

Peggy Lampl
Executive Director
Children's Defense Fund
Washington, D.C.

David M. Nee
Executive Director
Florence V. Burden Foundation
New York, New York

Barbara Price
Program Director
American Council of Life
  Insurance
Washington, D.C.

Congressman Edward Roybal
Chairman
Select Committee on Aging
U.S. House of Representatives
Washington, D.C.

Gerard L. Seelig
Executive Vice President
Allied-Signal, Inc.
Morristown, New Jersey

Humphrey Taylor
President and Chief Operating
  Officer
Louis Harris Associates
New York, New York

P. Michael Timpane
President
Teachers College
Columbia University
New York, New York

T. Franklin Williams, M.D.
Director
National Institute on Aging
Bethesda, Maryland

Contents

"The aging society is both a success and a challenge."

In Brief

ISSUES associated with the aging of America are best framed and analyzed if one bears in mind that

- the aging society is both a success and a challenge;

- the elderly population is greatly diversified;

- the relationship between individuals and generations is characterized essentially by interdependence and reciprocity;

- all generations have a common stake in social policies and intergenerational transfers that meet needs throughout the life course; and

- the nation's future *can* be changed and shaped by choices made today.

The Trends and the Challenge

More people are living longer, largely because of better sanitation, improved public health, and the control of life-threatening diseases. In 1900 life expectancy at birth was about 47 years for men and 49 years for women.* In 1985 it was an estimated 71.5 years for men and 78.8 years for women. About four out of five individuals can now expect to reach age 65, at which point—all things being equal—there is a better than 50 percent chance of living past 80. Moreover, for increasing numbers of elderly people, the quality of life is vastly improved over that for previous generations.

Both the increased probability of reaching old age and the generally improving quality of life in old age can be credited to the successful

---

*Citations for all data in this summary will be found in the end notes.

1

advances made by past and present generations in addressing problems across the life course, notably public and private investments in research, education, public health, social policies, and economic growth. These investments were often made in policies and programs having no apparent connection with the aged as well as in those that appear to serve only the elderly. For example, although programs that have all but eliminated many life-threatening infectious diseases may have been justified previously for their benefit to children and young adults, their success also accounts for the increasing numbers who survive to old age. Similarly, although Social Security provides income directly to retirees, it also benefits younger persons in many ways.

Still, as a society we must deal with the reality that millions of older people continue to live in or near poverty and continue to be afflicted with debilitating chronic illnesses. Further, we have to recognize that the large majority of the elderly who are not poor or who are not significantly limited in their normal activities—and even many who are— wish to maintain their autonomy, to contribute as much as they can to their families and communities, even in advanced old age. Thus, we are challenged to find ways to ensure the economic well-being of the elderly; to reduce the incidence, or delay the onset, of chronic illness; to provide humane care to those who require assistance or attention on a continuing basis; and to offer opportunities for the elderly to make productive contributions to society at large.

To meet the challenge of an increasingly aging society will naturally cost increasing sums of money. Unhappily, the challenge comes at a time of painful economic uncertainty. The nation faces a seemingly intractable federal-deficit problem. Sharp budget cuts in many government programs at all levels—federal, state, and local—have particularly impaired our ability to meet the needs of poor children, and demographic changes (e.g., growth in single-parent households and increasing participation of women in the work force) are limiting the time family members can spend providing direct care to the very young or to the functionally disabled of any age. Inevitably, questions press about the quantity and quality of opportunities available to younger generations, and about the impact of the federal deficit on these opportunities.

So the challenge of an aging society extends far beyond concerns about the quality of life for the elderly. It cries for a civic commitment to improve the quality of life for *all* members of society, regardless of age. At root, the challenge is inextricably linked to the need for economic growth and for full use of the nation's productive capacity.

Diversity of the Elderly

The outstanding characteristic of the elderly, now and in the future, is their diversity. In 1984 about a fourth of elderly families reported incomes of $30,000 or more, while one-fifth reported incomes under $10,000. Among elderly individuals, about 11 percent reported incomes of $20,000 or above while 25 percent reported incomes under $5000. At the same time, a substantial portion of the elderly occupy marginal economic status. In 1984 the incomes of 5.6 million elderly (21.2 percent) were below the near-poverty thresholds ($6,224 for a single elderly person and $7,853 for an elderly couple).

Although most noninstitutionalized elderly consider themselves to be in good or even excellent health, about one-fifth report limitations on their ability to carry on at least one major activity of daily living. Persons aged 85 and over are more than four times as likely as persons 65 to 74 to need in-home and institutional long-term care.

Understanding this diversity is critical if society is to assess accurately the various impacts of policies and proposed changes on particular groups of the elderly.

Interdependence and Reciprocity

The amount and type of resources individuals give and receive vary as they grow and age, generally in this sort of pattern: 1) in childhood individuals mainly receive resources; 2) throughout the young adult and middle years, they usually give more than they receive; and 3) in later years—particularly in advanced old age—they receive more and more resources even as they continue to give them. For any society to progress and prosper, each generation must provide assistance to, and receive assistance from, those that follow.

A comprehensive social policy, therefore, must focus not on a single moment in the life course—say, childhood or old age—but rather on the positions and needs of diverse individuals as they move through their lives. From such a perspective, the reciprocity of giving and receiving that goes on over time among individuals, and between generations, becomes a commanding principle. It is the bond of *interdependence* that ties society together. Prior experience thus emerges as an important determinant in the quality of life at all ages.

The Intergenerational Inequity Thesis

Regrettably, the current debate over the role of government in society has produced an approach that frames policy questions primarily in terms of competition and conflict between young and old. It is

3

grounded not in the interdependence of generations but in an assumption of intergenerational inequity, the rationale for which goes like this:

> Due to previous circumstances of the elderly and the broad-based perceptions of the elderly as both "needy" and "worthy," there has been a flow of public resources (income, health, and social services) toward the elderly, which has successfully improved their economic status and access to health care. In fact, the elderly are (or shortly will be) financially better off than the nonaged population. In light of this improved status, of large federal deficits, of the cost to younger persons of continuing present policies, and of anticipated growth of the elderly population, the flow of resources to the elderly seems "intergenerationally inequitable" and a source of intergenerational conflict.

While seemingly neutral in approach and possessing an intuitive appeal (who can be against fairness?), the argument carries with it very pessimistic views about the implications of an aging society. It would have us believe that

- programs for the elderly are a major cause of current budget deficits and economic problems;

- the elderly receive too large a portion of public social welfare expenditures to the detriment of children and other groups;

- because of demographic trends, the future costs of programs for the elderly will place an intolerable burden on younger workers; and

- younger people will not receive fair returns for their Social Security and Medicare investments.

As articulated thus far, the "intergenerational inequity" argument frames policy questions in terms of competition for scarce resources. It assumes that it is possible to measure accurately the fairness of the flows of resources between generations; that the amount of resources available for social programs in the future will and should be comparable to or less than what is currently available; and that advances in research, education, and economic growth will not change straightline projections of the need for future health care and retirement income, nor will they change projections of our collective ability to respond. The approach evaluates costs and benefits of social policies primarily at a single point in time, measures fairness in terms of dollars rather than outcomes, and draws many of its conclusions from comparisons between broad demographic groups such as "the elderly" and "children."

Flaws and Misunderstandings

Not only are many of these assumptions based on misunderstandings, but the analytic approach itself is flawed. For example:

1. *"Intergenerational inequity" does not take into account the overall dependency ratio.*

Many pessimistic arguments are based on the oft-referenced "aged dependency ratio," which measures the number of persons aged 65 and over (all of whom, for the purpose of this measure, are presumed "dependent") for every 100 persons aged 18 to 64 (all of whom are presumed to be contributing to the economy). Currently, there are 19 dependent elderly persons per every 100 persons of so-called "working ages." Using the definition above, the aged dependency ratio is projected to rise slowly to 22 persons in 2010 and then increase rather precipitously to 37 persons by 2030, leading some to conclude that the costs of programs for the elderly will be unsustainable unless drastic changes are made now.

This sounds ominous indeed, but the aged dependency ratio as described shows only part of the so-called "dependency burden." In contrast, the "overall dependency ratio," which measures the total number of persons under age 18 plus those aged 65 and over for every 100 persons aged 18 to 64, provides a very different picture. As economist Barbara Boyle Torrey points out, never at any time during the next 65 years is the overall dependency ratio projected to exceed the levels it attained in 1964. While it should be noted that the composition of governmental and private expenditures for younger and older Americans is quite different, clearly the overall dependency ratio does not paint quite so gloomy a picture about society's ability, through public and private mechanisms, to enhance the quality of life for persons of all ages.

Further, according to Brandeis University researcher William Crown, both the aged dependency ratio and the overall dependency ratio are flawed because they fail to take into account such factors as the increasing labor force participation of women, the potential for significant portions of the elderly to work longer, or the effect of economic growth. For example, when the midrange assumptions of the Social Security Administration about the growth of the economy and the size of the future U.S. population are used, real GNP per person is projected to nearly double by 2020 and triple by 2050. Barring unforeseen disasters, the economy of the future seems likely to be able to support a mix of programs for all age groups.

2. *"Intergenerational inequity" assumes that all the elderly are well off.*

Having discovered that all elderly are not poor, some journalists, academics, and policymakers have gone to the other extreme and declared that all elderly are financially comfortable, thereby justifying the position that public benefits should be reduced.

Failure to recognize the heterogeneity among the elderly—even among those aged 85 and over—leads to distortions in how social problems are defined, to misunderstandings about the implications of policy options, and ultimately to poor policy. Even so, these stereotypes persist, in part because stereotypical thinking is convenient, in part because negative attitudes about the elderly and growing old exist, and in part because, for some, stereotypes further political ends such as reducing social programs.

3. *"Intergenerational inequity" sees conflict as the rule.*

Conflict between generations is the exception, not the norm. Certainly, examples of conflict can be found, such as those showing the elderly voting against a school-related tax in a particular community. Care should be taken, however, not to conclude that conflict between generations is the "rule" or that the elderly are a cohesive political group intent on forcing their will against the interests of the young (or vice versa). Despite assertions of "senior power" by the press and by senior advocacy organizations themselves, political scientists such as Robert Binstock, Robert Hudson, and John Strate, who study the voting behavior of the elderly, generally conclude it is influenced far more by such things as lifelong party affiliation, social class, race, and political beliefs than by age. Opinion surveys show, too, that all age groups are willing to support programs for the elderly, particularly when given a choice between cutting defense spending or programs like Social Security and Medicare.

Considerable evidence also exists to show that the elderly are concerned about the needs of the young. In a 1983 poll commissioned by the American Council of Life Insurance, 88 percent of the elderly believed parents should feel a great deal or some responsibility to provide grown children with a college education, and 85 percent believed parents should feel a great deal or some responsibility to provide their grown children with a place to live if those children are unable to afford their own.

4. *"Intergenerational inequity" is based on a narrow view of fairness.*

Equity between generations, while certainly desirable, is a very limited criterion on which to base the distribution of scarce resources among those with competing claims. Even if all parties could agree on what constitutes a fair distribution of resources among generations, achieving such a balance would not necessarily meet many of the nation's goals for social justice. For example, it would not guarantee 1) that poor citizens would be provided with minimally adequate resources; 2) that nonpoor citizens would be protected from the risks of drastic reduction in their standards of living due to factors beyond their control; or 3) that all citizens would be afforded equal opportunity to achieve what their potentials allow. In short, as Binstock, a professor at Case Western Reserve University, has observed, the current preoccupation with equity between generations "blinds us to inequities within age groups and throughout our society."

Similarly flawed is the notion that per capita public expenditures on children and the elderly ought to be equal. Such an equation assumes that the relative needs of children and the elderly for public expenditures are identical and that equal expenditures are the equivalent of social justice. In fact, a sense of fairness based on the concept of need may require that greater per capita expenditures be directed at children than at the elderly, or that very substantial outlays of public resources be directed at certain subgroupings of children (for example, the growing number of children living in poverty), but not at others. Further, even if the aggregate needs of each group were the same, equal per capita expenditures directed at children and the elderly in the face of substantial unmet needs are not the same as social justice, nor would they result in equal outcomes.

It is sometimes argued that Social Security is unfair because today's young, as a group, will not have as high a rate of return on their "investments" in these programs as current retirees. Still others consider it "intergenerationally inequitable" that these programs do not function like private insurance programs, in which benefits are strictly related to the amount of contributions made.

The concept of fairness incorporated in such arguments is based on a misunderstanding of the multiple purposes of Social Security and Medicare. These goals include preventing economic insecurity through the sharing of risks against which very few could protect on their own, enhancing the dignity of beneficiaries, and providing stable financing. For example, to prevent economic insecurity, Social Security must provide a floor of protection through special provisions for low-wage workers and for certain family members, thereby emphasizing social adequacy. Once this goal is accepted, it is impossible to guarantee in addition that the rate of return for all parties will be identical.

5. *"Intergenerational inequity" uses limited measures to draw broad conclusions.*

Since each generation receives transfers from those that precede it and also gives transfers to those that follow, to reach accurate conclusions about equity between generations would require an examination within the context of the multiple intergenerational public and private transfers that are occurring constantly. Further, such an examination would have to answer questions like these:

How should the economic and social investments made by previous generations be valued? What about those of current ones?

Should part of what is spent on the elderly be counted as a return on *their* investments in younger generations? Should part of what is spent on children be considered an investment in future productivity?

How should investments made in research, conservation, environmental protection, and defense be allocated among generations?

Comprehensive measurement of intergenerational transfers is virtually impossible. As an alternative, analysts sometimes measure a particular resource transfer—for example, the percent of the federal budget directed at children versus the elderly. There is nothing necessarily wrong with making such measurements. What's wrong is to use them as the basis for broad and inappropriate conclusions about equity.

6. *"Intergenerational inequity" fails to recognize the common stake in social policies.*

By framing policy issues in terms of competition and conflict between generations, the intergenerational inequity perspective implies that public benefits to the elderly are a one-way flow from young to old and that there is no reciprocity between generations. This simply is not the case.

7. *"Intergenerational inequity" assumes a zero sum game.*

In accepting a framework that pits young against old over the division of scarce resources, the intergenerational inequity framework assumes a "fixed pie," which apparently can only be cut from one of two places—either the elderly or the young. By doing so, the framework takes for granted, wrongly, that the federal pie cannot be increased by economic growth or more tax revenues, and/or that the slice of pie for domestic programs cannot be increased as a result of reduced defense spending.

8. *"Intergenerational inequity" distracts attention from important policy issues.*

By framing issues in terms of trade-offs between young and old rather than in terms of policy goals or other trade-offs, the intergenerational inequity framework distracts attention from more useful ways of evaluating and making social policy. It also serves to deflect consideration of such important questions as 1) whether taxes should be raised; 2) whether the rapid growth and current composition of defense expenditures are in the national interest; and 3) whether new policies are needed to meet the needs of the most vulnerable citizens, regardless of age. Discussions about the unacceptably high rates of poverty among children, for instance, get obfuscated by the suggestion that declines in the elderly poverty rate are causally related to the precipitous increase in poverty among children—almost as if an increase in poverty among the elderly would somehow help children!

9. *"Intergenerational inequity" undermines the family.*

Were the inequity argument to be embraced as principle and used to justify government's lack of obligation to respond to the growing pressure on families for care-giving, many families could be overwhelmed by the stresses inherent in providing care for relatives. By promoting conflict, advocacy of such a principle might even subtly weaken the bonds between generations within the family.

While those who use this approach to policy-making span the political spectrum, some proponents see it simply as a convenient rationale for an ideology that opposes all public efforts directed at meeting family and individual needs. This point of view encourages attitudes that do not fully represent either the rich mix of values in our society or the balance generally sought between private and public solutions to social problems.

In Truth, the Generations Are Interdependent

Fairer and more effective social policy, we suggest, would be based on a tacit understanding of the interdependence of generations. This approach recognizes the heterogeneity of age groups within the U.S. population, evaluates costs and benefits of social policies primarily over time rather than at just one moment in time, and stresses the importance of understanding who—indirectly as well as directly—pays for and benefits from social policies existing and proposed. Finally, the approach takes a life course perspective to help explain the seeming paradox of the autonomy and interdependence of individuals and age groups as they move through life. Consequently, it emphasizes the importance of thinking broadly about how policies directed at one age group may affect all others—at any given point in time and over time—as these groups age. And it suggests that in an interdependent and aging society, all generations have a common stake in family efforts and public policies, or intergenerational transfers, that respond to the needs of people of all ages.

The Role of Intergenerational Transfers

Intergenerational transfers are not limited to government programs and public policies that transfer income and in-kind services (e.g., Social Security, education between generations). They also include private (e.g., family care-giving, inheritances) and societal (e.g., economic growth, new technology) transfers.

To consider only transfers resulting from public policies would be to miss a major way generations assist each other. Analysis that includes the value of housework and child care along with a few other nonmoney items (e.g., imputed rent from equity in a house) as part of the contribution made by individuals in families leads University of Michigan economist James Morgan to conclude that "the family is by far the most important welfare or redistributional mechanism even in an advanced industrial country like the United States with extensive public and private income maintenance programs"; he estimates transfers within families in 1979 to be $709 billion, equivalent to 30 percent of the gross national product.

Generations also assist each other through societal intergenerational transfers. These involve, for example, the legacy (e.g., economic growth, culture, values, knowledge) older generations bequeath to younger ones as well as the improvements (e.g., economic growth, new technology) younger generations make to the benefit of older ones.

There is no guarantee that particular birth cohorts or generations (within families) will receive more than they will give through intergenerational transfers, although generally this has been the case in American society. Without intergenerational transfers, however, the very continuity and progress of society and families would cease because needs that all experience at various points in life would not be met and legacies of the past would not be transmitted.

Currently, for children, especially the very young, the family is the principal provider. This is particularly true in this country because care-giving is a special domain of the family. As a child ages, the family generally remains dominant, although formal structures (especially educational institutions) become increasingly important. Farther along the life course, society has chosen to have government play a stronger role, especially through income maintenance and health care programs. Nevertheless, the family plays a significant role in offering assistance to the elderly who are functionally disabled.

Interdependence of generations within families. Ordinary care-giving and care-receiving exchanges occur within the family every day, ranging from assisting a spouse or child with a cold to paying for a college education. These exchanges are numerous, as exemplified by findings from a Harris survey that 1) more than four-fifths of family members aged 18 to 24 run errands for parents or grandparents and help them when someone is ill; and 2) even people aged 80 and over continue to provide support to younger generations in their families, with 57 percent helping out when someone is sick and 23 percent running errands. And some of these transfers involve financial resources; Urban Institute researcher Thomas Espenshade estimates that the cost of raising a typical child in a middle-class household to age 18 is $82,400 (in 1981 dollars).

Over the course of life, many persons will also give and/or receive extra-ordinary care. This might happen, for example, if a child is born with Down's syndrome, if a spouse becomes a paraplegic following an automobile accident, or if an aged parent or grandparent develops a chronic and seriously debilitating heart ailment.

It is primarily the family that is asked to respond when serious support needs arise and, in most cases, to bear most of the long-term costs. About 80 percent of elderly persons requiring assistance in the normal activities of daily life live in private settings. Most of the service these persons receive comes from family members, who provide such care for a number of reasons, including a sense of reciprocity, of filial responsibility, and of duty based on assistance previously provided by the older family members.

The costs to families of providing such care are likely to increase in the future as a result of the aging of society—especially the growth of the very old population—and other demographic trends. One set of projections suggests that the elderly long-term care population will increase from 6.6 million persons today to over 9 million by the year 2000, to nearly 13 million by 2020, and to nearly 19 million by 2040. Further, other social trends are straining the family's capacity to function as a provider of care. These trends include 1) increased rates of divorce and childbirth to unmarried persons, resulting in growing numbers of single-parent households; 2) increased participation of women in the labor force; and 3) the growing preference for smaller families, resulting in fewer children to share care-giving.

The real issue facing the nation, then, is not how to ask families to give more care across the life course with the intent of reducing public expenditures. Rather, given demographic trends, the crucial question is what kinds of assistance should be offered to help the family continue in its traditional care-giving role.

Long-Term Views of Social Programs

The interdependence of generations framework primarily bases its analysis on a longitudinal approach to evaluating costs and benefits of public policies. This approach examines the flow of tax payments and benefits over time. Thus, it is quite different from the cross-sectional approach emphasized by the intergenerational inequity framework, which examines the flow of tax payments and public benefits primarily at one moment in time. And it often leads to very different conclusions about who pays for and who benefits from such policies as public education, public health, investments made in research, Social Security, and Medicare.

Take public education as an example. From a cross-sectional perspective it would appear that education is primarily a transfer from working persons and other taxpayers to children and youth. From a longitudinal perspective, however, although the young clearly receive a transfer in the form of education, as they age they will also contribute to the education of those who follow as well as to economic growth and tax revenue, which will benefit the current workers as they age.

Social Security. As an outstanding example both of a program in which all generations have a common stake and of the importance of taking the long-term view of a social policy, consider Social Security. It serves these goals and values:

- the widespread preference for nonpersonal means of financial support in old age—that is, for the major responsibility for financial support of older relatives to be placed outside the family;

- the desire for a dignified and stable means of support for the elderly, the disabled, and surviving and financially dependent family members; and

- the need for a rational approach for protection against basic risks such as reduction of income due to retirement, disability, or death of a breadwinner.

The common stake in Social Security is also a result of the widespread distribution of benefits and costs among persons of all ages

To understand this common stake, it is not sufficient just to examine the direct benefits at one point in time—those that go primarily (about 85 percent), but not exclusively, to retired workers and their spouses, and to widows and widowers aged 60 and over. When time is "frozen" in this fashion, it may appear as if the distribution of burdens and benefits is unfair—with the young mostly paying and the elderly mostly taking. But identifying the direct and indirect benefits and the costs of Social Security over time presents a far different picture. The long-term perspective of Social Security shows that

- retirement benefits for today's younger workers will, on average, have greater purchasing power than those of today's retirees;

- Social Security introduces a critical element of stability into the retirement plans of young and middle-aged workers because even before benefits are first received, their value is kept up-to-date with rising wages and increases in the standard of living;

- disability and survivors protection alike have tangible worth to covered workers and their families;

- by providing cash benefits to older family members, Social Security frees up younger and middle-aged family members to concentrate more financial resources on their children; and

- by enabling family members and individuals to protect themselves against some major financial risks, Social Security stabilizes family life and the society.

Summary and Recommendation

These observations do not lead to the conclusion that such transfers are flawless and should never be changed. On the contrary, because of the basic functions they serve and because demographic and economic change is an ongoing process, policies should be reviewed carefully and options vigorously debated. Of critical importance now, however, is that those who are considering changes understand both who benefits from these policies and the common stake that prevails in these intergenerational transfers.

At best, the framing of issues in terms of competition and conflict between generations is based on a misunderstanding of relations between generations and distracts attention from more useful ways of examining social problems. At worst, it is a cynical and purposely divisive strategy put forth to justify and build political support for attacks on policies and reductions in programs that benefit all age groups. In contrast, we advocate an approach that assumes the interdepence of generations and emphasizes the importance of thinking broadly about how policies directed at one age group affect all others, at any given point in time and over time, as these groups age. Among our more important conclusions are these:

- It is erroneous to think of Social Security as a one-way flow of resources from young to old, or of education as a one-way flow from adults to children.

- The elderly, now and in the future, have at least two important stakes in programs that respond to the needs of children, young adults, and the middle-aged. First, they benefit directly and indirectly from education, training, and health programs that help increase the productivity of the work force. Second, it is in their political interest to pursue strategies that do not pit generations against each other.

- Younger generations have two important stakes in programs that assist the elderly to maintain a decent quality of life. First, they will be served by those programs when they become old. Second, such programs relieve young and middle-aged family members of financial burdens and intrafamily stresses.

- For both humanitarian and practical reasons, advocates for the elderly and others concerned with preparing for the retirement of the baby boomers have a special responsibility to support policies that respond to the needs and aspirations of the many poor and near-poor children in America. Failure to provide adequate educational, health, and employment opportunities to these children could undermine their future productivity and reduce the quality of life for the baby boomers during their retirement years.

Granted our preference for the interdependence framework, this report deals with a more basic issue—the importance of framing properly the policy debate necessary to meet the challenge of an aging society. Our single recommendation is that all those concerned understand the power of various frameworks to define the terms of this debate, and that they give careful consideration to the implications of each approach.

Ties That Bind

Authors' Preface

To MANY of us who had a hand in its preparation, this report merely documents the obvious. That the report is nevertheless needed cheers us not at all, for the controversy that motivated it is far more than a passing challenge to accepted wisdom. Cries of "intergenerational inequity" somehow violate the sense of social communion that most of us in this country absorbed with our baby food, and the implications are profoundly troubling.

What this report seeks to do primarily is to remind us of our common stake in intergenerational transfers. We state the case generally in chapter 1. Then, as background for the rest of the report, in chapter 2 we identify a few of the most important demographic trends related to the aging of America, as well as some of the key indicators of the economic status and health of the elderly. We describe the great diversity that exists among the elderly, review population trends, and note that choices made today will inevitably shape the well-being of our aging society tomorrow.

The three chapters that follow provide examples of the common stake. Chapter 3 shows the common stake in a private intergenerational transfer—the giving and receiving of care within the context of the family, including the interdependence of generations within the family and the reciprocal nature of exchanges that occur over the course of life. Even though care-giving is principally the family's function, we suggest a need for social policies that support and enhance the family's ability to give. Chapter 4 shows the common stake in an intergenerational transfer based on a public policy: Social Security. It discusses why a system built on social insurance principles allows much of the income support for the elderly to take place outside the family—an arrangement, judging from opinion polls, strongly preferred by the general public. The chapter also shows how, viewed long term, the benefits and costs of Social Security are distributed widely across all generations. Chapter 5 points up the common stake in what we call a societal intergenerational transfer. Using the example of public and private sector investments in research on aging, we suggest that such research is necessary to meet the challenge of an aging society and that all generations, especially younger ones, will benefit from the new knowledge that emerges from this investment.

The next two chapters illustrate how understanding the common stake in intergenerational transfers leads to a broader view of the implications of policies directed primarily at any one age group (e.g., children, youth, the middle-aged, or the elderly). Chapter 6 uses a life course perspective to discuss how quality of life in old age (indeed, at any age) is partially determined by prior experiences, and it suggests that each age group has a clear stake in social policies that will help shape their well-being at all points in the course of life. Chapter 7 builds on our understanding of the common stake and shows why advocates for the elderly, and the elderly themselves, have a stake in policies for children.

Chapter 8 identifies flaws in an approach to policy-making—the intergenerational inequity approach—that frames issues in terms of competition between young and old over the distribution of resources. This approach, we maintain, is based on a misunderstanding of several key concepts—namely, the implications of an aging society, the diversity of the elderly, and the common stake in intergenerational transfers—as well as on narrow measures of transfers of selected resources between generations to determine the fairness of public policies, and on an equally narrow interpretation of fairness. Application of this narrow interpretation to the policy process, we believe, could lead to several negative social outcomes, notably promoting conflict between generations and distracting attention away from more useful ways of evaluating and making social policy.

The report ends with a brief summary of the implications of applying the notion of the common stake to the policy process. In the afterword, we identify five broad research topics that must be addressed for a better understanding of intergenerational relations and the life course.

Ties That Bind: The Interdependence of Generations is the first in a series of reports on emerging issues in an aging society produced by The Gerontological Society of America. Its preparation was funded by the John A. Hartford Foundation, the AARP-Andrus Foundation, Allied-Signal, Inc., and the National Institute on Aging. Additional funding for dissemination of the report was provided by the American Association of Retired Persons.

Members of the society's Steering Committee, chaired by Professor Marjorie H. Cantor, were involved in every stage of the project, giving freely of their time and ideas. Members of the National Advisory Committee, chaired by Monsignor Charles J. Fahey, also shaped the project and reviewed drafts of the report, contributing their perspectives, insights, and creativity. The extraordinary commitment of both these committees, members of which are listed after the foreword, is greatly appreciated.

Robert H. Binstock, professor, Case Western Reserve University; Orville G. Brim, Jr., visiting scholar, Russell Sage Foundation; Boaz and Eva Kahana, professors, Case Western Reserve University; and James R. Storey, vice president of Chambers Associates, Inc., each provided useful suggestions as reviewers of the first draft. Able editing by Jane Gold greatly improved the manuscript. Many others who assisted are listed in the appendix.

The efforts of Sondra Shepard, the project assistant, were indispensable. Her outstanding organizational and word-processing skills made it possible to incorporate countless changes in the many drafts of the report. Linda Harootyan, director of information, provided constructive comments, including assistance on conceptualizing and organizing the report. Shirley Brown provided critical last-minute assistance and Adrian Walter provided helpful comments on drafts. Additionally, Betty Borgen, Nancy Carl, Charles Clary, Carol Cline, Pamela Dawson, Jean Francese, Jane Perino, Carol Schutz, and Jenny Youngdahl all lent valuable assistance to various aspects of the project.

And we would be remiss if we did not mention the support of our spouses: Joan Fernbach Kingson, Seth Hirshorn, and Donna Cornman; and our children—Aaron Kingson, age 4, Johanna Kingson, 1, Rebecca Hirshorn, 12, Rachel Hirshorn, 4, Geoffrey Cornman, 22, Jennifer Cornman 19, and Whitney Cornman, 17—who share, and are, our common stake in the future.

The views expressed in this report are those of the authors and not necessarily those of the Steering Committee or the National Advisory Committee. Nor do they represent official positions of The Gerontological Society of America.

Eric R. Kingson
Barbara A. Hirshorn
John M. Cornman

1

The Challenge
Of an Aging Society

THE AGING of our society is both a success story and a challenge. More people are living longer. The quality of life for increasing numbers of elderly* people is better than that for previous generations. Much of this progress can be attributed to public and private investments in successful research, in public policies, in education and public health programs, and in economic growth.

These investments were made by past and present generations, often in policies and programs having no apparent connection with the aged as well as in those that appear to serve only the elderly. For example, programs that have all but eliminated many life-threatening, infectious diseases may have been justified previously for their benefit to children and young adults, but their success also accounts for the increasing numbers who survive to old age. Similarly, Social Security provides income directly to retirees, but the program, as will be discussed later, also benefits younger persons in many ways. Further, these investments result in a growing opportunity for an aging society to use the talents and experience of the elderly.

In short, the increased probability of reaching old age and the generally improving quality of life in old age can be credited to all the successful investments and advances made by past and present generations in addressing problems across the life course. And indeed, these trends are important indicators of social progress.**

---

* Throughout this report the term *elderly* is used to refer to persons aged 65 and over; the *very old* refers to persons aged 85 and over.

**Of course, these are not the only indicators of social progress. Others would include economic growth, new knowledge, reduction and eradication of diseases, and reduction of poverty.

Yet, even while acknowledging the advances, we as a society must also recognize that millions of older people continue to live in or near poverty and continue to be afflicted with debilitating chronic illnesses. Further, the prevalence of poverty, chronic illness, and disability peak in the oldest age group, which is also the fastest growing segment of our population. Thus, as long as our society continues to value the lives of all individuals, the nation will be challenged to find ways to ensure the economic well-being of the elderly, to reduce the effects of chronic illnesses, and to provide humane care to those who require assistance or attention on a continuing basis.

However, no matter what breakthroughs biomedical research may achieve in preventing or treating chronic illnesses or how innovative new policies may be, it will cost money to meet the challenge of an aging society. In fact, because the size of the older population will continue to increase, the cost of meeting that challenge, both financial and otherwise, no doubt will also continue to increase—for individuals, families, and government.

Ironically, this challenge is occurring at a time when the nation is facing a serious federal deficit problem, and when the political mood of the country has encouraged dealing with this problem primarily by cutting federal domestic programs rather than by also increasing taxation and/or significantly reducing the growth of the defense budget. At the same time, poverty rates for children are very high, with more than one-fifth of children under age 18 (21.3 percent in 1984)[1] officially defined as poor. Complicating the situation is the reality that federal, state, and local programs designed to respond to the needs of poor children and their families have experienced a disproportionate share of budget cuts. Moreover, other social changes (e.g., growth in single-parent households, increasing labor force participation of women) are limiting the amount of time family members can devote to providing direct care to the very young or to the functionally disabled of any age.

The challenge is also occurring at a time when the oldest members of the baby boom generation, a generation considerably larger than those that precede or follow it, are but 25 years from retirement. Whatever the costs of meeting the challenge might have been with a more normal increase in the number of elderly, they will be multiplied as the baby boom generation moves into retirement. Moreover, the increasing life expectancy of persons at 65 and even 85 will augment the growth of the older population.

Finally, the challenge is occurring at a time of economic change

21

and deepening anxiety. More and more questions are being asked about the quantity and quality of opportunities available to younger generations in the future, and about the impact of a worsening federal debt on these opportunities.

In response to such pressures, interest groups have geared up to protest specific program cuts and are tempted to compete among themselves for a share of what is perceived to be a shrinking pie. Persons long opposed to many of the nation's social welfare policies use the debt problem as a reason to increase their attacks. And some members of younger generations, perhaps fearing their opportunities for success will be limited, question the fairness of current policies, resource allocations, and economic conditions.

THE PURPOSE OF THE REPORT

In this context has emerged an approach to assessing social policies based on a loosely defined concept of "intergenerational inequity." This approach uses measures of transfers of selected resources between generations—intergenerational transfers—as a basis for determining the "fairness" of, and for making changes in, public policies. Framing policy questions in terms of competition between generations over scarce resources, this view is frequently invoked to justify charges that the elderly are receiving an inequitable share of public resources and that this inequity is sparking conflict between generations. Thus, while the concept of intergenerational inequity seems neutral in approach and possesses an intuitive appeal (who can be against fairness?), its application—whether by design or inadvertence—carries with it a very pessimistic view about the implications of an aging society, leading to particular policy goals and prescriptions.

The tone and character of the debate generated by this approach prompted the decision to prepare this report. The outcome of this debate could determine how our society reacts to the challenge of an aging society—from policies affecting children to policies affecting older persons; from the shape of research agendas to the design of income maintenance, educational, social service, and health care programs. Further, the debate is currently being conducted with such emotional rhetoric as to threaten some important aspects of the common wisdom that holds this country together: an appreciation of the basic values that have driven social policies in the past, a recognition of the diversity within all age groups, and an understanding that each generation contributes to and benefits from social progress.

For these reasons, we believe it important to put forth our view why, in an interdependent and aging society, all generations have a common stake in family efforts and social programs that respond to the needs of people of all ages. It must be emphasized that intergenerational transfers are not simply government programs or transfers that are the result of public policy (e.g., Social Security, education), but include a host of private efforts (assistance provided within families and the private sector) as well as wide-ranging societal transfers (e.g., economic growth, new knowledge). Society must now begin to think broadly about how policies directed at one age group may affect all others, at any given point in time and over time, as these groups age.

The purpose of this report, then, is not to advocate particular policies for meeting the challenge of an aging society. Rather, the intent is to 1) note the power of policy frameworks to shape debate over the implications of the aging of America; 2) emphasize the importance of thinking about society and the life course as a whole; 3) discuss the stake all generations have in private and public intergenerational transfers; 4) stress the importance of all levels of government sharing with individuals and families the burden of meeting the needs of persons of all ages; and 5) identify the implications, misunderstandings, and flaws of an approach to policy that, based on a narrow interpretation of equity between generations, frames policy issues in terms of competition and conflict between generations. While we recognize the challenge of an aging society, we are more optimistic about the nation's ability to respond to this challenge without compromising the needs of any citizens, regardless of age. This view, we believe, is consonant with the traditional values and realities of American family life.*

UNDERSTANDING THE COMMON STAKE

Our view that all generations have a common stake in private and public intergenerational transfers that respond to human needs across the life course is based on an understanding of

- the high degree of interdependence between individuals and between generations within society,

- the implications of the life course perspective for public policy,

- the role of private and public intergenerational transfers in society, and

---

*For a description of how the report is organized, see Authors' Preface.

- a long-term view of the distribution of benefits and costs of social policies.

The Interdependence of Individuals and Generations

We live in a highly interdependent society in which it is both expected and normal for individuals to have needs throughout their lives that can only be met by other individuals or social institutions. Infants depend for their survival on parents and others; children need adequate education to become productive adults; adults generally need others for their livelihood; and persons who are ill often need assistance from friends, family, professionals and/or medical institutions. Thus, while it is generally understood that children, persons with significant health problems, and the elderly—especially those who are ill or otherwise limited—need assistance, it is also true that needs exist at all points in the life course, even for the seemingly self-sufficient. As former Social Security commissioner Robert Ball points out:

> a businessman to be successful . . . has to have customers, roads, railroads, airplanes and . . . employees who have been to school. The amount he adds to all this is important but he can't go it alone. He didn't earn it all by himself. [2]

A person's needs vary in degree and mix over time. Some can be met by informal support from individuals and families; others require the assistance provided through social institutions. Further, at any given point in time, most individuals generally *both give and receive* help. The probability of being more on the receiving than on the giving end changes over the course of life and varies from person to person.

The reciprocity of giving and receiving is the bond of *interdependence* that links members of society together. Interdependence is a primary means by which the needs of all members of society are met. Further, this interdependence extends between generations.* For society to continue and progress, each generation must provide assistance to and receive it from the one that follows. Again, as Ball observes:

> We owe much of what we are to the past. We all stand on the shoulders of generations that came before. They built the schools and established the ideals of an educated society. They wrote the books, developed the scientific ways of thinking,

---

*Use of the term *generation* is explained further on in this chapter under the heading *What Is Generation?* (see p. 31).

passed on ethical and spiritual values, discovered our country, developed it, won its freedom, held it together, cleared its forests, built its railroads and factories and invented new technology. . . .

Because we owe so much to the past, we all have the obligation to try to pass on a world to the next generation which is a little better than the one we inherited so that those who come after, standing on our shoulders, can see a little further and do a little better in their turn.[3]

Implications of the Life Course Perspective*

As the previous discussion suggests, an understanding of the common stake in intergenerational transfers also rests on the life course perspective. Rather than simply focusing on one moment in time (e.g., childhood or old age), this perspective examines individuals and their needs throughout their entire lives.

The amount and type of resources individuals give and receive vary as they move through life's stages, generally in the following pattern: 1) in childhood individuals mainly receive resources; 2) throughout the young adult and middle years, individuals usually give more than they receive; and 3) in later years—particularly in advanced old age—individuals increasingly receive resources but often still give them as well. For instance, a study conducted by University of Michigan economist James N. Morgan shows it is mainly middle-aged family members who assist friends or relatives not in their immediate families by giving one or more of the following: time or money in an emergency, regular financial support, or housing. The same study shows

---

*The life course perspective is sometimes referred to as the "life span" or "life cycle" perspective, and it provides the basis for much social science research on human development and aging. Central to it is the dual notion that there is continuity to a person's life and that a person has the ability to change throughout the life course.[4] The ways in which our lives are characterized by both continuity with our pasts and ongoing change are related to how personal circumstances (e.g., abilities, when we were born and to whom) interact with and are shaped by social structure (e.g., how society distributes rewards), historical events (e.g., war), and social policy. Although many factors that influence human development (e.g., new technologies) are largely outside our immediate control, we neither are nor become simply passive responses to society. Within the constraints imposed by society, we actively shape our lives through personal decisions and through decisions that in turn shape the society. This life course perspective also incorporates the idea that each "new birth cohort potentially ages through a different trajectory of life events, brought about by the impress of sociohistorical change and by individual reactions to it."[5]

Chart 1.1
Giving or Getting Assistance, by Age

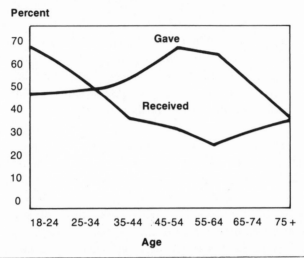

Percent

Gave

Received

18-24 25-34 35-44 45-54 55-64 65-74 75 +

Age

Source: James N. Morgan, "The Redistribution of Income by Families and Institutions and Emergency Help Patterns," in *Five Thousand American Families: Patterns of Economic Progress*, vol. 10, *Analyses of the First Thirteen Years of the Panel Study of Income Dynamics*, ed. Greg J. Duncan and James N. Morgan (Ann Arbor, Mich.: Institute for Social Research, University of Michigan, 1983).

it is mostly the young and the very old who receive such assistance (see chart 1.1).[6]

The life course perspective clarifies the reciprocity of giving and receiving that exists between individuals and generations over time. It also suggests that quality of life at all ages is related to prior experiences, which, in turn, implies 1) that quality of life in old age for current and future generations of the elderly is shaped by policies directed at *all* age groups, and 2) that each generation has a clear stake in policies that will shape its well-being at all points throughout the course of life. In short, the life course perspective points to the risks involved in focusing narrowly on the momentary interests of any particular generation and underlines the importance of examining policy interventions in terms of the entire life course and the needs of society as a whole.

The Role of Intergenerational Transfers

As noted previously, intergenerational transfers are responses of an interdependent society to needs that occur throughout life. Once again, it is important to understand that these transfers are not simply govern-

Chart 1.2
Illustrations of intergenerational transfers likely to be given and received over the course of life by different groups *

	Intergenerational transfers given					Intergenerational transfers received				
	Children 0-15	Youth 16-22	Adults	Elderly 65	Functionally disabled	Children 0-15	Youth 16-22	Adults	Elderly 65	Functionally disabled
Private transfers Child care	*	■	*			■	■			
Adult care	*	■	*					*	*	■
Family financial support		■	*			■	■	*	*	*
Inheritances			■	*		*	*	*		
Public transfers Education		*	*		*	■	■			*
Social Security		■	*		*	*	*	*	■	■
Health care programs		■	*			*	*	*	■	■
Public infrastructure		■	*	*		*	*	*	*	*
Societal transfers Economic growth	*	■	*			*	*	*	*	*
Knowledge, technology		*	*	*		*	*	*	*	*
Culture	*	*	*	*		*	*	*	*	*
Environment		*	*			*	*	*	*	*
National defense	*	*	*			*	*	*	*	*

* Identifies transfer received or given.   ■ Identifies transfer targeted on a particular group or for which the provider makes a particular contribution.

* This chart provides illustrations in intergenerational tranfers typically given and received over the course of life. Clearly there is much variation within each of the groups listed and so the chart should be viewed as simply presenting broad generalizations.

ment programs and public policies that transfer income and in-kind services (e.g., Social Security, education) between generations; they are also private and societal as well. (See chart 1.2 for illustrations of these three types.)

To overlook the role of the family and other private means of transferring resources between generations would be to miss a major way generations assist each other. Analysis that includes the value of housework and child care along with a few other nonmoney items (e.g., imputed rent from equity in a house) as part of the contribution made by individuals in families leads Morgan to conclude that ''the family is by far the most important welfare or redistributional mechanism even in an advanced industrial country like the United States with extensive public and private income maintenance programs.''[7] Assigning a value to housework and child care of $6 an hour, Morgan estimates transfers within families in 1979 to be $709 billion—equivalent to 30 percent of the gross national product (GNP).[8]

Although the primary focus of this report is on private intergenerational transfers and those that result from public policy, it is important to recognize the role of societal intergenerational transfers. These involve, for example, the legacy (e.g., economic growth, culture, values, knowledge) older generations bequeath to younger ones as well as the improvements (e.g., economic growth, new technology) younger generations make to the benefit of older ones.

There is no guarantee that particular birth cohorts* or generations within families will receive more than they will give through intergenerational transfers, although generally this has been the case in American society. However, without such transfers, the very continuity and progress of society and families would cease because needs that all experience at various points in life would not be met and legacies of the past would not be transmitted. Thus, it is clear that the tradition of providing intergenerational transfers through the family, the private sector, and the government rests on more than just self-interest. In discussing the philosophy of Social Security, J. Douglas Brown refers to an implied covenant arising from a deeply embedded sense of mutual responsibility in a civilization.[9] Based on the idea that those within a family who can work should assist those who cannot, this covenant is key to understanding not only Social Security or public school education, but all public and private intergenerational transfers.

The lifetime pattern of need establishes, to a large extent, the age groups most in need of receiving resource transfers and the providers most able to supply them. For society to survive and progress, it is essential that resources be transferred from those who are producing goods and services (including homemaking) to those whose needs go beyond the goods and services they currently produce for themselves. One way or another, such transfers must and will be made. The extent to which they are made through the family, government, or other mechanism (e.g., private insurance) is largely a matter of social custom, historical circumstance, and economic efficiency of service delivery.

Currently, for children, especially the very young, the family is the principal provider. This is partly because care-giving is a special domain of the family (see chap. 3) and because the public seeks to limit government involvement in the nuclear family. As the child ages, the

---

*The term *birth cohort* is defined further on in this chapter under the heading *What Is Generation?* (see p. 31).

28

family generally remains dominant, although formal structures (especially educational institutions) become increasingly important. For reasons discussed elsewhere in the report (see chap. 4), our society has chosen to have government play a stronger role—especially through income maintenance and health care programs—in meeting the needs of the elderly. But it is well known that, when available, families play a significant role in assisting the elderly who are functionally disabled (see chap. 3).[10]

Because of both the way need varies throughout people's lives and the relative roles government and the family play in response, the preponderance of intergenerational transfers at any one point in time is from working-age adults to children and the elderly, with the family being the primary source of transfers for children and the government for the elderly. Over time, however, as individuals and birth cohorts age—thereby passing through various stages of need—they are clearly involved in both giving and receiving.

A Long-Term View of the Benefits and Costs of Social Policies

Our understanding of the common stake in public policies that generate intergenerational transfers is based on a long-term view of how benefits and costs of social policies are distributed. This perspective identifies both the direct and indirect benefits of social policies and examines the costs of such policies over time.

To begin with, it is important to understand that distribution of the costs and benefits of social policies among different age groups can be analyzed in two different ways, leading to very different conclusions.[11]

Cross-sectional analysis, which, for example, examines the flow of Social Security tax payments and benefits *at one moment in time*, emphasizes that current workers pay taxes while the elderly are the primary beneficiaries. From this perspective it appears that the young are mostly giving and the elderly mostly taking. On the other hand, *longitudinal* analysis, which examines the flow of tax payments and benefits *over time*, emphasizes that not only do current workers pay taxes but, as their birth cohorts age, they can expect to be the future beneficiaries of Social Security—assuming the institution remains stable. And from this perspective, current beneficiaries have contributed—either through their own or through a family member's tax payments—to the benefits they receive and to the stability of the institution. Similarly, from a cross-sectional perspective, it would appear that education is primarily a transfer from working persons and other taxpayers to the young. From a longitudinal perspective, however, although the young clearly receive a transfer in the form of education, as they age they will also contribute to the education of those who follow.

Identifying the indirect as well as the direct benefits and costs of social policies may also alter conclusions reached about who benefits from and who pays for particular policies. Using education again as an example, the immediate *direct* benefits clearly accrue to children; however, the numerous *indirect* benefits go to working parents who do not need to arrange for child care during school hours, to teachers hired to educate the young, and to all who will benefit from the future productivity of an educated work force.

Summary of the Common Stake

The main points to be kept in mind throughout this report are these:

• The United States is a highly interdependent society in that it is both expected and normal for individuals to have needs throughout their lives that can only be met by other individuals or social institutions.

• People have varying degrees and mixes of needs at any given moment in their lives.

• Individuals and generations are generally on both the giving and receiving ends of assistance, though the extent to which they are giving or receiving will generally vary over the life course.

• Intergenerational transfers are public and private responses to needs occurring across the life cycle and are two-way flows from and to birth cohorts and individuals over their lifetimes.

• Intergenerational transfers include transfers of personal services, knowledge, culture, technology, economic growth, and biomedical advances, as well as cash and in-kind benefits.

• Intergenerational transfers are crucial to the continuity and progress of individuals and society.

• An understanding of who benefits from and who pays for social policies requires analysis from both a cross-sectional and a longitudinal perspective, as well as identification of both direct and indirect benefits and costs.

Before discussing the demography of our aging society, we would like to alert the reader:

• We reject an approach to policy-making based on loosely defined concepts of intergenerational inequity.

• The term *generation* is used in a variety of ways and is rather difficult to define precisely.

• Analysis of social policy issues—such as those included in this report—involve, to a significant extent, examinations of social values.

Clarifying Our Concerns About Intergenerational Inequity

Importantly, our objections to particular interpretations of equity between generations as an approach to policy-making (or as a slogan) should not be confused with opposition to a fair (equitable) society. We are *not* opposing the goal of fairness—either in society or between generations—although we must confess that, after studying the concept of intergenerational inequity for over a year, we are not convinced it has been clearly defined in policy discussions. Our problem with this concept is that it is quite flawed and uses narrow definitions of fairness (equity) to draw broad and highly questionable conclusions about what is fair.

What Is Generation?

Since the term *generation* is used by journalists, academics, and the general public in many ways, it is important to differentiate among its several meanings and to explain how we use the term.

Age group. Sometimes an age group is referred to as a *generation*. Age groups are classifications made according to age (e.g., persons under 19 are often classified as children).

Birth cohort. More commonly, *generation* is used to describe a birth cohort (e.g., the baby boom generation). Birth cohort (also called *age cohort* or simply *cohort*) refers to persons born at roughly the same interval of time[12]—often measured within 10- or 20-year intervals (e.g., the cohort born in the 1930s). Members of a birth cohort move through time together. As birth cohorts age, they move into different age groups (e.g., from advanced middle age into old age).[13] Finally, *generation* is also used to refer to a self-conscious group or subgroup of a birth cohort that may share a common set of concerns and political goals (e.g., "the rebellious generation of youth of the 1960s").[14]

Lineage within families. In addition to the above meanings, *generation* is sometimes used to refer to lines of descent—that is, lineage within families (e.g., grandparents, parents, children).[15]

In this report, we frequently use *generation* as a catch-all term for age group, birth cohort, or lineage within families. Where appropriate, however, we distinguish between different uses of the term.

Social Policy and Social Values

Although not always recognized as such, social policies reflect society's basic value commitments, and policymakers "are often in the position of recommending or making precedent-setting decisions involving fundamental values."[16] Consequently, examinations of social policy and policy options, such as those included in this report, are largely discussions of social values.

As the United States considers the options that will ultimately shape the future of public and private intergenerational transfers in an aging society, it is essential to recognize that policy choices inevitably involve compromises and trade-offs among cherished but conflicting values. Use of a narrow framework that emphasizes only one value, or a limited set of values (or goals), is likely to lead to policy outcomes that

- provide simplistic answers for complex questions,

- severely compromise other equally cherished values that are not recognized, and

- have unintended and undesirable long-term impacts.

We do not try to identify all the values affirmed and/or compromised when social policy issues are framed in terms of either of the two approaches outlined above. Such an undertaking is beyond our scope here. Instead, throughout this report we identify some of the major values emphasized both by the intergenerational inequity view of social policy, which suggests that generations are in conflict over the distribution of scarce resources, and by our view, which suggests that all generations have a common stake in intergenerational transfers.

And finally, in preparing the report, we do not mean to suggest that no current policy or program should be changed. Indeed, demographic pressures, shifting economic conditions, biomedical advances, and new technologies will force policy changes. But as we struggle to respond to such pressures and to find an effective mix of policies that will allow all age groups in our society and future generations to continue to progress over time, we believe that decision makers, advocates, and the general public ought to keep in mind how various policy options and approaches to policy would affect long-held societal values and goals and, indeed, the fabric of our society.

At the same time, while the report does not advocate particular policies or values, we do not pretend to approach our task without assumptions or biases. So that the reader may understand the basis from which we proceed, we list the most important of those assumptions, which are that our society, at least in theory (and, we hope, in fact), will continue to

- value each individual's life;

- be concerned with improving the quality of life for all its members;

- value the rights and obligations of individuals to participate in making decisions affecting their lives;

- value the involvement of individuals, families, and government in meeting the needs of people, while continuing to debate the mix of these reponsibilities; and

- be concerned with increasing, maintaining, or extending the autonomy of all citizens as an important societal goal.

Notes

1. Bureau of the Census, "Money Income and Poverty Status of Families and Persons in the United States: 1984" (advance data from the March 1985 *Current Population Survey*), *Current Population Reports*, ser. P-60, no. 149 (Washington, D.C.: U.S. GPO, August 1985), 3.

2. Robert M. Ball, Commencement Address (University of Maryland-Baltimore County, Catonsville, Md., 9 June 1985).

3. Ibid.

4. Orville G. Brim, Jr., and Jerome Kagan, "Constancy and Change: A View of the Issues," in *Constancy and Change in Human Development*, ed. Orville G. Brim, Jr., and Jerome Kagan (Cambridge, Mass.: Harvard University Press, 1980), 1-25.

5. David L. Featherman, "The Life-Span Perspective in Social Science Research," in *Behavioral and Social Research: A National Resource*, ed. R. McAdams et al. (Washington, D.C.: National Academy of Sciences, 1982), 622.

6. James N. Morgan, "The Redistribution of Income by Families and Institutions and Emergency Help Patterns," in *Five Thousand American Families: Patterns of Economic Progress*, vol. 10, *Analyses of the First Thirteen Years of the Panel Study of Income Dynamics*, ed. Greg J. Duncan and James N. Morgan (Ann Arbor, Mich.: Institute for Social Research, University of Michigan, 1983), 16.

7. Ibid., 2.

8. Ibid., 11.

9. J. Douglas Brown, *Essays on Social Security* (Princeton, N.J.: Princeton University Press, 1977), 31-32.

10. Elaine M. Brody, "Parent Care as a Normative Family Stress," *The Gerontologist* 25 (February 1985); Marjorie Cantor and Virginia Little, "Aging and Social Care," in *Handbook of Aging and the Social Sciences*, ed. Robert H. Binstock and Ethel Shanas, 2d ed. (New York: Van Nostrand Reinhold Co., 1985).

11. Our discussion of the implications of taking a cross-sectional or longitudinal view of how Social Security benefits and costs are distributed draws heavily on Norman Daniels, "Justice Between Age Groups: Am I My Parents' Keeper?" *Milbank Memorial Fund Quarterly/Health and Society* 61, no. 3 (n.d.).

12. Nathan W. Shock et al., *Normal Human Aging: The Baltimore Longitudinal Study of Aging* (Washington, D.C.: U.S. GPO, 1984), 5.

13. Our discussion of the distinction between birth cohorts and age groups draws on Daniels, "Justice Between Age Groups."

14. Vern L. Bengston et al., "Generations, Cohorts, and Relations Between Age Groups," in *Handbook of Aging and the Social Sciences*, ed. Binstock and Shanas, 2d ed., 307.

15. Ibid.

16. John Tropman, "Value Conflicts and Policy Decisionmaking: Analysis and Resolution," *Human Systems Management* 4 (1984): 215.

2

The Aging of America

THE AGING of our society is characterized by two principal factors: demographic changes in our population and the diversity of the elderly.

The growth of the elderly. The elderly (i.e., the population aged 65 and over) have grown and will continue to grow both in numbers and as a percent of the total population, although it is important to note that the anticipated rate of growth is not uniform (see chart 2.1). Whereas in 1900 only 3 million persons—4 percent of the population—were elderly, today there are about 29 million—representing 12 percent of the population. Between now and the year 2000, the Census Bureau estimates modest growth in the numbers (to about 35 million) and percent (to about 13 percent) of the elderly population. Beginning around 2010, when the first of the baby boom generation reaches age 65, the elderly population will begin to swell so that by 2030—the height of that generation's retirement—an estimated 65 million persons (about 21 percent of the population) will be elderly. After that, the rate of increase in the numbers of elderly is expected to slow considerably, with the elderly population projected at 73 million in 2080.*[1]

The rapid growth of the very old. The very old (that is, the population aged 85 and over) are anticipated to grow even more rapidly than the elderly population as a whole (see chart 2.1). Whereas today 2.7 million persons are 85 and over (1.1 percent of the entire population), the Census Bureau estimates that this population group will grow to 4.9 million (1.8 percent) in 2000, 8.6 million (2.8 percent) in 2030,

---

*See chapter 8 for a discussion of the changing aged and overall dependency ratios.

Chart 2.1
Population 65 Years and Over by Age: 1900–2050

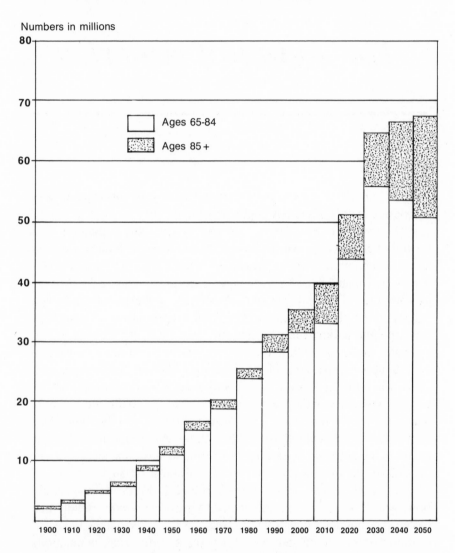

Numbers in millions

Ages 65-84

Ages 85+

Sources: Bureau of the Census, "U.S. Census of Population 1890–1980," and "Projections of the Population of the United States, by Age, Sex, and Race: 1983–2080," *Current Population Reports*, ser. P-25, no. 952, middle series (Washington, D.C.: U.S. GPO, 1984).

and 16 million (5.2 percent) in 2050 when all the survivors of the baby boom generation will be 85 or older.[2]

Expanding life expectancies. Due largely to improved sanitation, improved public health, and the control of life-threatening (especially childhood) diseases, life expectancy at birth increased very rapidly in the United States during the first half of the twentieth century—from about 47 years for men and 49 years for women in 1900 to about 66 and 71 years, respectively, in 1950 (see table 2.1).[3] Since 1950, life expectancy at birth has increased to an estimated 71.5 years for men and 78.8 years for women in 1985. Social Security's actuaries estimate that life expectancy at birth will increase to 76.9 years for men and 84.6 years for women by 2060.[4]

Most improvements in life expectancy in the second half of this century and projected for the next are and will be the result of improvements in life expectancy at age 65. Whereas life expectancy at age 65

Table 2.1
Past and Projected Life Expectancy at Birth and at Age 65, 1940 to 2060*

| | Life Expectancy | | | |
| | At Birth | | At Age 65 | |
Calendar Year	Male	Female	Male	Female
1940	61.4	65.7	11.9	13.4
1950	65.6	71.1	12.8	15.1
1960	66.7	73.2	12.9	15.9
1970	67.1	74.9	13.1	17.1
1980	69.9	77.5	14.0	18.4
1985	71.5	78.8	14.7	19.1
1990	72.6	79.8	15.1	19.8
2000	73.9	81.2	15.8	20.7
2010	74.5	81.8	16.1	21.1
2020	75.0	82.3	16.5	21.6
2030	75.5	82.9	16.8	22.0
2040	76.0	83.5	17.2	22.5
2050	76.4	84.0	17.6	23.0
2060	76.9	84.6	17.9	23.4

*The projected life expectancies for 1985 to 2060 are based on the intermediate demographic assumptions used in the Board of Trustees *1985 Annual Report.*

Source: Board of Trustees, Federal Old-Age and Survivors Insurance and Disability Insurance Trust Funds, *1985 Annual Report of the Federal Old-Age and Survivors Insurance and Disability Insurance Trust Funds* (Washington, D.C.: U.S. GPO, 1985).

in 1940 was 11.9 years for men and 13.4 years for women, today it is estimated at 14.7 and 19.1 years, respectively; by 2010 at 16.1 and 21.1 years; and by 2050 at 17.6 and 23.0 years, respectively.[5]

Elderly women outnumber elderly men. Due to the higher rates of death among men, there are today three elderly women for every two elderly men. This represents a significant change since 1960 when there were five elderly women for every four elderly men. Among the very old, the disparity is even greater, with one hundred women for every forty-three men (see chart 2.2).[6] Moreover, given both the above differences in sex ratios at the older ages and traditional marriage patterns, it is not surprising that elderly women, especially the very old, are far less likely than elderly men to be living with a spouse. Today, 82 percent of men aged 65 to 74 and 70 percent of men aged 75 and over live with a spouse, compared with only 49 percent of women aged 65 to 74 and 22 percent of women aged 75 and over. These differences in the numbers and marital status of men and women have significant implications. For example, elderly women are generally at greater risk of not having adequate income or assistance available in the home in the event of a disabling health condition.

Chart 2.2
Number of Men Per 100 Women by Elderly Age Group, 1984

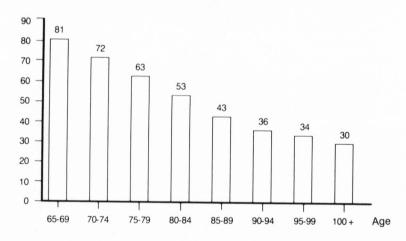

Source: Bureau of the Census, "Projections of the Population of the United States, by Age, Sex, and Race: 1983–2080," *Current Populations Reports*, ser. P-25, no. 952, estimates (Washington, D.C.: U.S. GPO, 1984).

Significance of the aging of America. As discussed in chapter 1, these trends represent both a success story and a challenge. For the society, they indicate that the investments made by past and present generations in economic growth, public health, and successful public policies have resulted in more people living longer. For the individual, they mean that about four out of five people can expect to reach age 65, at which point there is—all things being equal—a better than 50 percent chance of living past age 80.

Some, however, have interpreted this success as a reason for pessimism about the future. They argue that the changing age composition of the society will result in unsustainable burdens on future cohorts of younger workers. This simply is not the case.

The challenge of an aging society can be met. From the individual's viewpoint, the challenge is to increase the probability for a good quality of life in old age through such efforts as careful financial planning, proper nutrition, preventive health care, exercise, and involvement in productive activities (e.g., employment, volunteer work, maintenance of property, hobbies). For society, however, the real challenge is to 1) increase the likelihood that the extra years being added to life are generally worth living; 2) better utilize the skills and knowledge of the elderly; 3) meet the income and health care needs of the elderly; and 4) do all this within the context of improving the quality of life for *all* members of society, regardless of age.

The Diversity of the Elderly

The outstanding characteristic of the elderly, now and in the future, is their diversity (heterogeneity). This diversity encompasses a multitude of characteristics—from economic, work, and health status to race, gender, and even age—since at any given time "the elderly" consist of several birth cohorts. Thus, there is little profit in painting the older population with too broad a brush. Indeed, the older population is really composed of many different groups with vastly different needs, and it is important that policies designed to meet their needs take this differentiation into consideration instead of responding to a generalized portrait of the "typical older person."

Income trends and status.[7] Since the early 1960s, the economic status of the elderly has, in general, greatly improved as measured by declines in the poverty rate and increases in income (after adjusting for inflation). Very substantial declines occurred in the poverty rate among the elderly between 1959 and 1974—from 35.2 percent to 14.6 percent. Since 1974, it has been relatively stable—ranging between 14 per-

Chart 2.3
Poverty Rates for Nonaged and Aged
1966–84

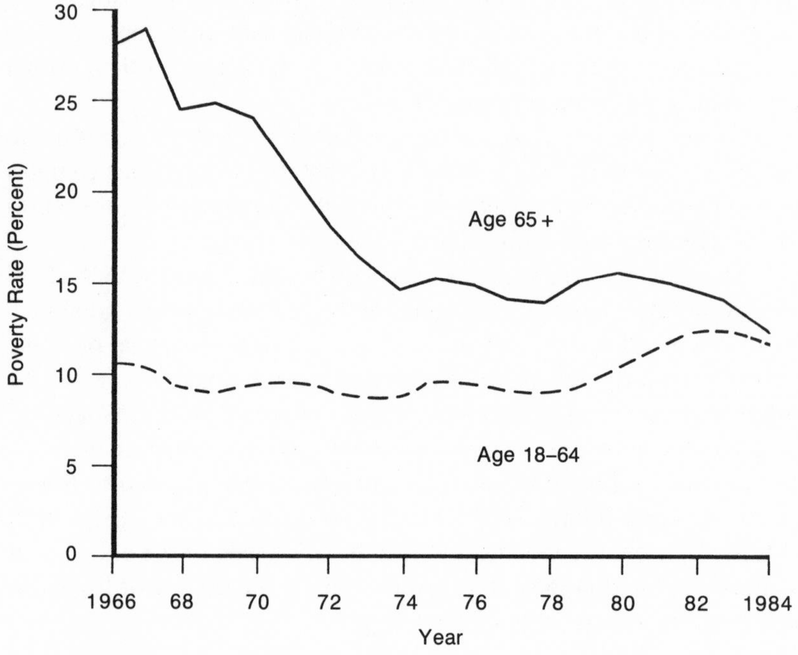

Source: Bureau of the Census, *Current Population Surveys*, 1967–85.

cent and 15.7 percent for most of the period and declining to 12.4 percent in 1984 (see chart 2.3 in which poverty trends of the elderly are compared with those of adults aged 18 to 64). At that time, the poverty rate of the elderly was lower than that of the total population (14.4 percent), but higher than that of adults aged 18 to 64 (11.7 percent).[8]

The economic welfare of the elderly, as measured by trends in median income, has also improved both in real terms (i.e., after adjusting for inflation) and in relation to the total population (see table 2.2).[9] In addition, the incomes of the elderly today are generally well protected against inflation, while in-kind income such as Medicare and Medicaid and the use of consumer durables such as homes also exert a positive influence on the economic well-being of the elderly.[10]

Much of this improvement results from expanded protections under Social Security. Much is also due to the economic growth of the past

Table 2.2
Median Family Income, 1965–84,
Elderly and Nonelderly Families

Year	Median Family Income (actual dollars)			Median Family Income (1984 dollars)	
	Head Aged 25 to 64	Head Aged 65 +	CPI	Head Aged 25 to 64	Head Aged 65 +
1965	$ 7,537	$ 3,460	94.5	$24,822	$11,396
1966	8,146	3,645	97.2	26,083	11,671
1967	8,753	3,928	100.0	27,242	12,225
1968	9,511	4,592	104.2	28,408	13,715
1969	10,438	4,803	109.8	29,587	13,614
1970	10,879	5,053	116.3	29,113	13,522
1971	11,406	5,453	121.3	29,266	13,991
1972	12,717	5,968	125.3	31,587	14,824
1973	13,496	6,426	133.1	31,558	15,027
1974	14,380	7,505	147.7	30,301	15,814
1975	15,331	8,057	161.2	29,599	15,555
1976	16,624	8,721	170.5	30,345	15,919
1977	17,960	9,110	181.5	30,798	15,622
1978	19,764	10,141	195.4	31,480	16,153
1979	22,175	11,318	217.4	31,746	16,203
1980	23,392	12,881	246.8	29,499	16,244
1981	25,138	14,335	272.4	28,721	16,378
1982	26,003	16,118	289.1	27,993	17,351
1983	27,243	16,862	298.4	28,414	17,587
1984	29,292	18,236	311.1	29,292	18,236

Source: Bureau of the Census, *Current Population Reports*, ser. p–60. 1965–83, and unpublished data from the 1985 *Current Population Surveys*.

Note: CPI (Consumer Price Index) figures establish a baseline (100) of the costs of goods and services in 1967, against which price increases and decreases can be measured. Consumer prices in 1979, for example, were more than double the prices in 1967 for the same goods and services (217.4 compared to 100). The Census Bureau revised its method for imputing interest income when calculating 1984 income levies in order to correct an historical bias which underestimated missing interst income data. Data in Table 3-9 for 1965–83 were computed under the earlier methodology, while 1984 median family income levels were calculated using the revised method.

35 years, which has enabled new cohorts of the elderly to reach old age with higher levels of Social Security income, greater probability of having other retirement income, and more valuable assets (especially home equity).

Today, the major sources of cash income for the elderly are Social Security (accounting for 39 percent of all their income), assets (25 percent), earnings (18 percent), and other income such as private or public-employee pensions (14 percent) (see chart 2.4). The centrality of Social Security as a source of income is illustrated by data provided by the Social Security Administration, which indicate that nearly three-fifths

Chart 2.4
Income Sources for Aged Units 65 and Older,
1982

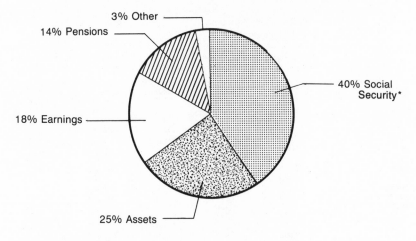

3% Other

14% Pensions

40% Social
Security*

18% Earnings

25% Assets

* Includes Social Security and railroad retirement. Railroad retirement accounts for about 1 percent of income for aged units.

Source: Grad, Susan, *Income of the Population 55 and Over,* Social Security Administration, 1982.

of elderly households reported in 1984 that Social Security provided at least half of all their income. In particular, lower and moderate income households reported that a large portion of their income is from Social Security, with, for example, Social Security providing a little more than 70 percent of the total income going to the approximately 11 million elderly households reporting incomes under $10,000 in 1982.[11] Consequently, the economic security of elderly households—especially those of low and modest income—is very sensitive to changes in Social Security.

While it is important to recognize the generally improved economic status of the elderly, it is also important to note that they have less financial flexibility.[12] As a consequence, their economic well-being is more vulnerable to risks such as those associated with the cost of chronic illnesses.

Diversity of economic circumstances. Economic circumstances among the elderly vary widely. For instance, in 1984 one-fifth of elderly families reported incomes under $10,000, while one-quarter reported incomes of $30,000 or above. Among elderly individuals, 25 percent reported incomes under $5,000 and about 11 percent reported incomes of $20,000 or above.[13] In fact, the distribution of money income is more unequal among the elderly than among the nonelderly.

Clearly, while some elderly are very well-off and others modestly so, a substantial portion remains whose economic status is marginal at best. For instance, in 1984 some 5.6 million (21.2 percent) were classified as near poor—that is, below the near-poverty thresholds ($6,224 for a single elderly person and $7,853 for an elderly couple in 1984).[14] Further disaggregation of the income statistics shows that certain groups of the elderly—namely widows, the very old, and minorities—have very high poverty rates. For example, about 22 percent of all elderly Hispanics, 32 percent of all elderly blacks, 20 percent of elderly unmarried white women, and 57 percent of elderly black women living alone had below-poverty incomes in 1984.[15] Similarly, disaggregation of median income figures shows that in 1982, "elderly white men aged 65 to 69 had median incomes of about $11,900; white women, $5,700; black men, $5,900; and black women, $3,900."[16] Finally, when the incomes of the elderly are broken down by age, the very old generally have the lowest incomes (see chart 2.5).

Chart 2.5
Median Elderly Family Income by Age, 1983

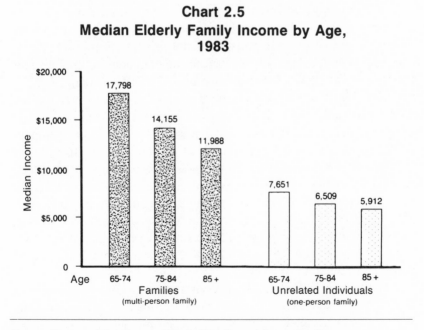

Source: Bureau of the Census, March 1984 *Current Population Survey*.

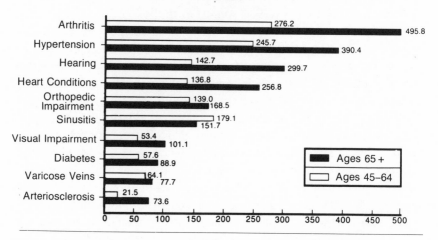

Chart 2.6

**Top 10 Chronic Conditions for the Elderly—
Rates Per 1,000 Persons,
1982**

Condition	Ages 45–64	Ages 65+
Arthritis	276.2	495.8
Hypertension	245.7	390.4
Hearing	142.7	299.7
Heart Conditions	136.8	256.8
Orthopedic Impairment	139.0	168.5
Sinusitis	179.1	151.7
Visual Impairment	53.4	101.1
Diabetes	57.6	88.9
Varicose Veins	64.1	77.7
Arteriosclerosis	21.5	73.6

■ Ages 65 +
□ Ages 45–64

Source: National Center for Health Statistics, Health Interview Survey, 1982

Health status. Although the vast majority of the elderly experience at least one chronic health problem, most of the noninstitutionalized elderly (about 65 percent) consider themselves to be in good or even excellent health, while only 19 percent report poor health that limits their ability to carry on at least one major activity of daily living.[17]

The elderly experience far more chronic conditions than the rest of the population (see chart 2.6). For example, arthritis affects an estimated 50 percent, hypertensive disease 39 percent, hearing impairments 30 percent, and heart conditions 26 percent (see chart 2.6).

Primarily because of their higher rates of chronic illness, the elderly necessarily use health care more than other groups,[18] accounting for nearly one-third of the nation's health care expenditures. However, although government programs pay for a substantial portion of the health care of the elderly (see chart 2.7), approximately one-fourth of the elderly's health care costs are paid for out-of-pocket—averaging about 15 percent of their total income.[19]

While most of the elderly function independently, the probability of declining health and a consequent need for greater assistance increases with age. For instance, while at any given time only about 5 percent of the elderly reside in nursing homes, it is estimated that persons who

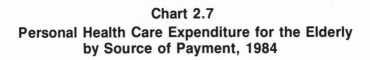

Chart 2.7
Personal Health Care Expenditure for the Elderly
by Source of Payment, 1984

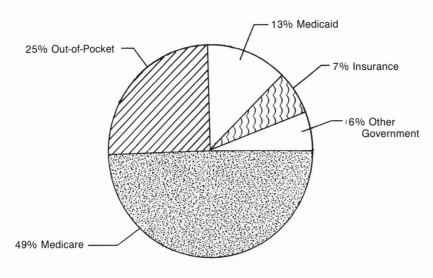

25% Out-of-Pocket

13% Medicaid

7% Insurance

6% Other Government

49% Medicare

Source: Health Care Financing Administration, Office of Financial and Actuarial Analysis.

reach age 65 have an approximately 50 percent chance of spending some time in a nursing home.[20]

While Medicare has greatly increased access for the elderly to hospital-based and physician services for acute illnesses, it provides relatively little support for long-term care services. Medicaid provides considerable support for institutional-based long-term care services but relatively little support for those long-term care services provided in the community. Research has shown that the great bulk of noninstitutional care of the functionally disabled elderly is provided by family members[21]—spouses (usually wives), children (usually daughters or daughters-in-law), and siblings. This care serves as the cornerstone of community-based long-term care. As Elaine Brody of the Philadelphia Geriatric Center noted in testimony before the House Committee on Aging:

> It is *not* true as the stubborn myth would have it that "families nowadays do not take care of their old as they did in the past." To the contrary, *families nowadays provide more care, more*

difficult care, over longer periods of time to more older people than ever was the case before. This despite the fact that family caregivers nowadays have fewer personal resources with which to provide that care and are confronted with more competing demands on their time and energy.[22]

Plainly, as the numbers of the elderly grow and their average age increases, there will be more need for both community- and institutional-based long-term care services (see chap. 3 for expanded discussion).

Diversity of health status among the elderly. As with economic well-being, the diversity of health status among the elderly is quite striking. This can be seen when the need for in-home and institutional long-term care services is described according to different age groups among the elderly: persons aged 85 and over are more than four times as likely as persons aged 65 to 74 to need such services (see chart 2.8).[23]

While most elderly can perform daily activities (e.g., dressing, bathing, eating, toileting) without assistance, it is estimated that 6.7 percent of persons aged 65 to 74, 15.7 percent of persons aged 75 to 84, and fully 39.3 percent of those aged 85 and over need help from another person to perform one or more of these activities.[24]

Chart 2.8
Percent of Population Aged 65+ in Need of Long-Term Care Services, 1980

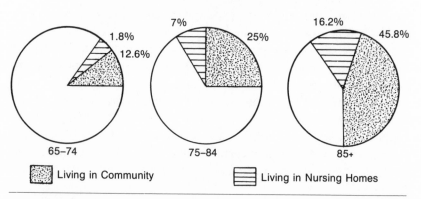

Source: Kenneth G. Manton and Korbin Liu, "The Future Growth of the Long-Term Care Population: Projection Based on 1977 National Nursing Home Survey and the 1982 Long-Term Care Survey," as cited in Senate Special Committee on Aging, *Developments in Aging: 1984*, 99th Cong., 1st sess., 28 February 1985, S. Rept. 99-5, 188.

Health status also varies considerably by sex. Elderly women generally have higher rates of most chronic illnesses than do elderly men, although the diseases that are more common to men are more life-threatening.[25] Similarly, reported health status among the elderly varies by income status, with the higher-income elderly generally reporting better health than other elderly persons (see chart 2.9).

The health status of elderly minorities is generally poorer than that of elderly whites. For example, information from the National Health Interview Surveys indicates that about 57 percent of elderly blacks compared with 44 percent of elderly whites report some limitation in activity due to chronic conditions.[26] There is also considerable diversity by race and ethnicity in terms of survival to and in old age. In 1982, for

Chart 2.9
Self-Assessment of Health by Income Range:
Persons 65 and Older*
1981

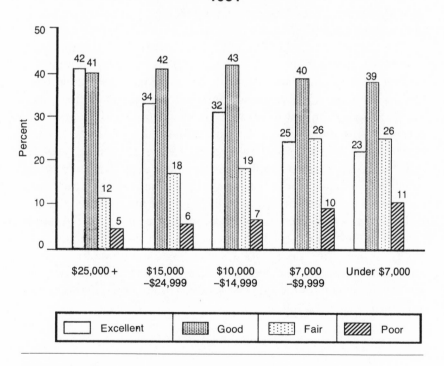

Source: National Center for Health Statistics. Health Interview Survey 1981.

*Figures may not total 100 percent due to rounding.

example, 12 percent of whites were aged 65 or older, as compared with 8 percent of blacks, 6 percent of Asians and Pacific Islanders, and only 5 percent of American Indians and Hispanics.[27] Moreover, *within* the age ranges of the older population is a further race-related distinction: nonwhites appear to have higher death rates at lower ages, and whites appear to have higher death rates at higher ages. For instance, "the death rates of Blacks exceed those for Whites at age 65 to 69, 70 to 74, and 75 to 79, but from ages 80 to 84 and higher," nonwhites have lower death rates than whites.[28]

Understanding the diversity of the elderly. We have emphasized the heterogeneity of the elderly because stereotypes of this age group—as either all rich or all poor, all healthy or all ill, all retiring voluntarily or all retiring involuntarily—do not provide a realistic basis for policy-making. Similarly, consideration of this diversity is critical if society is to assess accurately the various impacts of policies and proposed changes on particular groups of the elderly. Further, an appreciation for the diversity among the elderly should foster a similar appreciation for the diversity among other population groups such as children and the middle-aged. An understanding of this is basic to an effective policy for an aging society.

And finally, in thinking about the trends associated with the aging of America, it also is important to remember that the future is mutable, ready to be shaped or changed by the choices we make today. Far from holding the future hostage, the demographic, health, and income trends identified today are just a few among several factors (including also current events and economic growth) influencing our ability to meet the challenge of an aging society. Thus, it does not automatically follow that, because per capita health care costs have been escalating in the recent past, they will continue to do so. Or that nursing home beds need to increase in direct proportion to the aging of the population, especially the growth of the very old. Or, for that matter, that the retirement of the baby boomers need place undue strains on the economy's ability to meet their needs. As a society we can choose to invest in research or not; to encourage employment of elderly Americans in old age or not; to plan for the aging of America or not. The paths we chart today will shape the future.

Notes

1. Bureau of the Census, "Projections of the Population of the United States, by Age, Sex, and Race: 1983-2080," *Current Population Reports*, ser. P-25, no. 952 (Washington, D.C.: U.S. GPO, 1984), 2-9.

2. Ibid., 7-9.

3. Board of Trustees, Federal Old-Age and Survivors Insurance and Disability Insurance Trust Funds, *1985 Annual Report of the Board of Trustees of the Federal Old-Age and Survivors Insurance and Disability Insurance Trust Funds* (hereafter referred to as Board of Trustees, *1985 Annual Report*) (Washington, D.C.: U.S. GPO, 1985), 30.

4. Ibid.

5. Ibid.

6. Senate Special Committee on Aging, in conjunction with the American Association of Retired Persons (hereafter referred to as AARP), the Federal Council on Aging, and the Administration on Aging, *Aging America: Trends and Projections 1985-1986* (Washington, D.C.: U.S. GPO, 1985), 19; U.S. Congress, Office of Technology Assessment (hereafter referred to as OTA), *Technology and Aging in America*, OTA-BA-264 (Washington, D.C., June 1985), 279.

7. This discussion of income trends and status relies on data from Current Population Surveys (CPS). These surveys of households are conducted by the Bureau of the Census. The survey data serve as a basis for a series of reports issued by the bureau on incomes and poverty rates of Americans and for a series of reports published by the Social Security Administration on the income of the population aged 55 and over. A recent study has estimated that the CPS is subject to underreporting error (about 11 percent)—especially at higher income levels—largely because property income is likely to be substantially underreported (see Daniel B. Radner, "Distribution of Family Income: Improved Estimates," *Social Security Bulletin* 45, no. 7 [n.d.]: 13-21). Primarily because of underreported property income and secondarily because of unreported earnings, the underreporting among the elderly appears to be greater than that among other adults. If adjustments were made for this problem, the relative importance of Social Security as a source of income for the elderly would decline somewhat, particularly at higher income levels.

8. Senate Special Committee on Aging, *Aging America: Trends and Projections 1985-1986*, 43; Bureau of the Census, "Money Income and Poverty Status: 1984," 21-23.

9. Yung-Ping Chen, "Economic Status of the Aging," in *Handbook of Aging and the Social Sciences*, ed. Binstock and Shanas, 2d ed., 645-646.

10. Robert L. Clark et al., *Inflation and the Economic Well-Being of the Elderly* (Baltimore, Md.: The Johns Hopkins University Press, 1985), 120-121; James H. Schulz, *The Economics of Aging*, 3d ed. (Belmont, Calif.: Wadsworth Publishing Co., 1985), 40-44.

11. Unpublished data, Social Security Administration, Office of Research, Statistics and International Policy; Susan Grad, *Income of the Population 55 and Over, 1982*, prepared for the Social Security Administration (Washington, D.C.: U.S. GPO, 1984), 66, 74, 80.

12. James Storey, Chambers Associates, Inc., personal communication, Washington, D.C., 4 November 1985.

13. Bureau of the Census, "Money Income and Poverty Status: 1984."

14. Ibid.

15. Senate Special Committee on Aging, *Aging America: Trends and Projections 1985-1986*, 53.

16. Senate Special Committee on Aging, *Developments in Aging: 1983*, 98th Cong., 2d sess., 29 February 1984, S. Rept. 98-360, 26.

17. Senate Special Committee on Aging, *Aging America: Trends and Projections 1985-1986*, 84-86.

18. Robert L. Kane and Rosalie A. Kane, School of Public Health, University of Minnesota, personal communication, 12 November 1985; Senate Special Committee on Aging, *Aging America: Trends and Projections 1985-1986*, 84.

19. Senate Special Committee on Aging, *Aging America: Trends and Projections 1985-1986*, 106.

20. It has been widely reported that about 25% of persons who reach age 65 will spend some time in a nursing home. More recent analysis suggests that the "elderly individual's risk of institutionalization approaches and may exceed 50%." For a review of the literature, a discussion of the relative merits of techniques of estimating this risk, and a presentation of findings based on a life table method of estimation, see Charles E. McConnel, "A Note on the Lifetime Risk of Nursing Home Residency," *The Gerontologist* 24 (April 1984): 196-197.

21. Brody, "Parent Care"; Cantor and Little, "Aging and Social Care"; Ethel Shanas, "The Family as a Social Support System in Old Age," *The Gerontologist* 19 (April 1979).

22. Elaine M. Brody, "Health Care Cost-Containment: Are America's Aged Protected," testimony before the House Select Committee on Aging, 9 July 1985, 2.

23. Senate Special Committee on Aging, *Developments in Aging: 1984*, 99th Cong., 1st sess., 28 February 1985, S. Rept. 99-5, 188.

24. Senate Special Committee on Aging and AARP, *Aging America: Trends and Projections* (Washington, D.C.: AARP, 1984), 63.

25. L. M. Verbrugge, "Women and Men: Mortality and Health of Older People," in *Aging in Society: Selected Reviews of Recent Research*, ed. M.W. Riley, B.B. Hess, and K. Bond (Hillsdale, N.J.: Lawrence Erlbaum Associates, 1983), as cited in Beth J. Soldo and Kenneth G. Manton, "Demographic Challenges for Socioeconomic Planning," *Socio-Economic Planning Science* 19, no. 4 (n.d.): 234.

26. National Center for Health Statistics, *Health Indicators for Hispanic, Black, and White Americans*, ser. 10, no. 148 (Washington, D.C.: U.S. GPO, 1984), 50.

27. Bureau of the Census, "America in Transition: An Aging Society," *Current Population Reports*, ser. P-23, no. 128 (Washington, D.C.: U.S. GPO, 1983), 4.

28. Bureau of the Census, "Demographic and Socioeconomic Aspects of Aging in the United States," *Current Population Reports*, ser. P-23, no. 138 (Washington, D.C.: U.S. GPO, 1984), 49.

3

The Common Stake In Family Care-Giving

CARE-GIVING within the family is the best example of a private inter-generational transfer, for several reasons. The exchange is common, accepted, and preferred; it occurs across the life course; it exemplifies the strong bonds between generations; and it demonstrates the difficulty of measuring intergenerational transfers to determine "inequities."

From birth onward, most individuals will both receive care from and give care to family members, unless disability or illness prevents or hampers them from serving as care-givers. Moreover, families share a wide range of intergenerational relationships and resources (e.g., time, money, thought, sheer physical energy) as part of their care-giving and care-receiving interchange. Thus, although a one-to-one reciprocity between family members is unlikely in either the kind or amount of care given or received, the exchange of care is so common and natural in our lives that we hardly notice much of it taking place unless and until it ceases. To understand the broad spectrum of care provided by families, it is helpful to think in terms of ordinary and extra-ordinary exchanges of care.

Ordinary Family Care-Giving and Care-Receiving
Over the Life Course

Regardless of the educational level, socioeconomic status, religion, or ethnic identity of a family's members, many quite ordinary care-giving and care-receiving exchanges occur within the family every day. Some exchanges are short term and discrete, such as tending to a youngster's broken arm; some are of a few years' duration, such as diapering a baby or sending a young person through college; and some last much longer, such as preparing breakfast for one's spouse regularly for most of one's married life. Ordinary exchanges of care can provide both maintenance support—including financial assistance, help with the chores of daily living (baby-sitting, shopping, fixing things in the home), and gift giving—and/or emotional support—including advice on such things as bringing up children or making a major purchase, and expressions of affection, approval, or consolation through visits and telephone conversations.[1]

Over most of the life course, family members typically give care to many of the same relatives from whom they receive it; thus, the ordinary exchange of care is frequently two-directional. Moreover, this care is exchanged not just between the generations in a family but also between particular people in the same generation.

In a national survey conducted during the mid-1970s by Louis Harris and Associates, Inc., respondents identified intergenerational exchanges between people over age 65 and younger family members. The report summarizing the survey states:

> The public 65 and over make it clear that they perform some valuable functions for the younger generation: 90% of those with children or grandchildren said that they "give gifts" to them, 68% "help out when someone is ill," 54% "take care of grandchildren," 45% "help out with money," 39% "give general advice on how to deal with life's problems," 34% "shop or run errands," 26% "fix things around the house or keep house for them," 23% "give advice on bringing up children," 21% "give advice on running a home," 20% "give advice on jobs or business matters," and 16% "take grandchildren, nieces or nephews into their home to live with them."[2]

Even people 75 to 84 and those 85 and older, who are more likely to be on the receiving end of the care exchange, continue to provide care-giving support to younger generations—their children, grandchildren, and often great-grandchildren. The report concludes:

> . . . among those 80 and over, substantial numbers continue to help out in a variety of ways: 86% say they give gifts, for example, 57% help out when someone is ill, 38% help out with money, 34% take care of grandchildren, 23% shop or run errands, and 20% fix things around the house. In ad-

dition, substantial numbers of those 80 and over give their
offspring advice on dealing with life's problems, bringing
up children, running a home, etc.[3]

The survey also found that younger family members (respondents
from 18 to 64 years of age) provide ordinary care-giving support for
older family members (parents or grandparents) (see table 3.1). For
example, nearly everyone in all age groups queried gave gifts to their
parents or grandparents; approximately four out of five helped out when
a parent or grandparent was ill; and two-thirds or more shopped or ran
errands for them.

Additional studies that have focused on intergenerational care
exchanges within families of more narrowly defined groups of Americans
(e.g., inner-city populations, ethnic groups) make many of the same
points as do evaluations of the U.S. population as a whole.*

Some analysts have tried to measure the flow of resources, under
ordinary circumstances, from parents who are young adults and middle-

Table 3.1
Percent of Persons Providing Various Services
to Parents or Grandparents, by Age

Service to Older Relatives	Age			
	18-24	25-39	40-54	55-64
Give gifts	96	92	95	95
Help out when someone is ill	81	70	81	78
Shop or run errands	84	65	76	71
Take them places	69	56	68	65
Help fix things around the house or keep house for them	65	60	65	57
Give advice on how to deal with some of life's problems	28	31	57	39
Help out with money	24	25	46	30
Give advice on money matters	15	23	47	47
Give advice on running home	11	12	28	22
Give advice on job/business matters	12	13	25	22

Source: Louis Harris and Associates, Inc., *The Myth and Reality of Aging in America*
(Washington, D.C.: National Council on the Aging, Inc., 1975), 73-74.

---

*See, for example, studies of family care-giving exchanges among the subpopula-
tions of both New York's inner city and Los Angeles.[4]

aged to their young and teen-aged children. Thomas Espenshade of the Urban Institute estimates that the parents of "the typical child in middle America . . . are likely to spend $82,400 to rear a child to age 18" (expressed in terms of 1981 price levels for a family of median socioeconomic status, two children, and a wife who works part time).[5] The cost of feeding a child, under these circumstances, would be $9,200 for those 18 years; shelter would cost approximately $7,500, clothing $6,000, and health care $4,700.[6] Thus, in addition to time and effort, ordinary care-giving often requires significant financial expenditure.

Clearly, then, the everyday exchange of ordinary care among family members underscores the interdependence of people. Moreover, family members usually *want* to depend on one another in receiving this care and *want to be depended on* for giving it.

Extra-Ordinary Family Care-Giving and Care-Receiving Over the Life Course

In addition, many persons will also give and/or receive extra-ordinary care. This might happen, for example, if a child is born with Down's syndrome, if a spouse becomes a paraplegic following an automobile accident, or if an aged parent or grandparent develops a chronic and seriously debilitating heart ailment.

While intergenerational exchanges of extra-ordinary care also take place daily, they are usually responses to support needs that are more demanding than most everyday needs. The opportunity to provide such support is rarely sought after, and when it comes, it quickly and radically alters family life, perhaps for a lifetime. However, when faced with circumstances requiring extra-ordinary care, the family usually responds as best as it can for as long as it can, for the most part providing both emotional and maintenance support.

Frequently, giving emotional support means assisting the stricken individual to come to terms with illness or disability, an adjustment that includes learning to live with one's pain, discomfort, and altered physical appearance and capabilities, as well as with one's new identity as a person who is much more frequently receiving care than giving it. Individual family members also find themselves providing emotional support to other members struggling to cope with this sudden, great demand to provide extra-ordinary care.

As for maintenance support, families involved in extra-ordinary care-giving can find themselves carrying out a whole new set of tasks— such as assistance with walking, dressing, bathing, and often even toileting—to help the stricken individual perform basic daily functions.

They also may find themselves involved in more minor tasks—such as making telephone calls or going to the bank, store, or library—that enable the sick person to maintain contact with the outside world. Moreover, in cases where patterns of family care-giving and care-receiving are altered radically by these extra-ordinary circumstances, families must try to establish new support exchanges that take into consideration not only the new responsibilities but also all the ordinary, everyday ones that address the needs of healthy family members.

For the most part, then, it is primarily the family that is asked to respond when serious support needs arise and, in most cases, to bear most of the on-going costs. Recognizing the support the family usually provides in such circumstances, as well as the innumerable, ordinary care-giving and care-receiving exchanges that take place among family members daily, promotes a better appreciation both of the intergenerational exchanges that take place within families and of the stake *all* generations in our society have in maintaining the family's ability to provide care for its members.

We next explore why families are willing to provide extra-ordinary care and some stresses they may encounter when they do. We do so by examining a particular kind of extra-ordinary family care—long-term care of older family members—which may well become a reality for increasing numbers of families at some time during the next several decades.

MOTIVATIONS AND STRESSES INVOLVED IN EXTRA-ORDINARY CARE-GIVING

Older family members in need of long-term care often have both given care to, and received care from, family members over the course of their lives. While some of the approximately 5.2 million older persons with chronic illnesses or disabilities currently living in the community experience only moderate limitations and thus need minimal assistance from family members, those with more severe functional limitations that leave them homebound, and possibly even bedfast, require considerably more assistance.[7] At this point in the course of their lives such individuals are primarily on the receiving end.

The amount and intensity of emotional and maintenance support an elderly family member needs can be substantial. Yet, as when faced with other kinds of extra-ordinary care-giving responsibilities, families usually accept the task and provide the best care they can. The duration of this support may be as long as is necessary, or it may be until the family can no longer provide the requisite skills or financial support or can no longer handle the situation emotionally. At this point, it must turn to outside sources for relief.

Factors Motivating Families to Provide Long-Term Care

Different researchers give a wide range of answers to the question of why families go to the effort—sometimes extreme—of providing this kind of care. To summarize them briefly:

Continuity of generations. When family members show they care for the survival and quality of life of all generations in a family, including the older ones, they may be reaffirming a sense of family that is more than just a passing on of genetic information and learned behavior, as it is with other animal species. Such caring may reflect a more expanded notion of family life that recognizes the importance of continuity across generations.

This recognition is demonstrated by children and grandchildren *wanting to provide* this care and seeing their older relatives *wanting to receive* it from them. At the same time, these younger generations *learn to want* and *expect* such care in the future from their own children and grandchildren. Thus, there is an expectation that the intergenerational exchange of care will persist over time to preserve not only the continued existence of one particular older family member but also the importance of the older generations to family life.

Reciprocity. The concept of care as a resource both given and received over the entire course of life implies a reciprocity between family members. As the studies mentioned earlier in this chapter illustrate, reciprocity of emotional and maintenance support between *healthy* older family members and members of the other generations in a family is substantial.

However, the pattern of exchange may differ markedly when the older family member requires family support for a chronic illness or disability. In this situation, according to analysts Amy Horowitz and Lois Shindelman:

> Reciprocity is conceptualized as stemming from the "credits" earned *by* the older persons for past help given to the caregivers. It is an obligation which stems from gratitude and is manifested in the desire to repay the older relative for past services rendered.[8]

Thus, an older person needing long-term care may go to family members for support because these are the people the older person helped in the past.*

Filial responsibility. Somewhat related to perceptions of what it means to reciprocate in this intergenerational exchange is the value placed on "filial responsibility." While there is some historical precedent in both Far Eastern and some Western history for filial responsibility toward the old as a tradition, there are two reasons why filial responsibility is fairly new as a major motivation for intergenerational care-giving. First, until the advent of an aging society, relatively few families were faced with the question of providing care for older people. And second, until the end of the nineteenth century, older family members owned the means of production (farms, farm equipment, etc.) until death, which made intergenerational relations more a question of economic survival than of filial responsibility. However, industrialization at the turn of the century took the means of economic survival out of the hands of parents. The decision to take care of elderly family members thus changed from one of necessity to one of choice, and the value of filial responsibility grew in importance as a motivation for intergenerational care-giving.[10] Today it appears to be a strong factor behind family care-giving behavior. For example, in one recent study that explored what three generations of women believe to constitute appropriate filial behavior toward elderly widowed mothers, researchers Elaine Brody, Pauline Johnsen, and Mark Fulcomer report that "large majorities of each generation indicated that adult children—regardless of gender, marital status, or work status—should adjust their family schedules ...when needed."[11] Elsewhere, Brody further notes:

> At some level of awareness, members of all generations may harbor the expectation that the devotion and care given by the young parent to the infant and child—that total, primordial commitment which is the original paradigm for caregiving to those who are dependent—should be reciprocated and the indebtedness repaid in kind when the parent, having grown old, becomes dependent.

---

*Moreover, although exact reciprocity between two family members is impossible over the life course, how much one "collects" often depends on how much one gave at an earlier time to the person from whom support is now requested. Horowitz and Shindelman also report that "caregivers do respond with more assistance the more they believe they have received in the past. Past behavior on the part of older relatives, therefore, does act as 'credits earned' which can be activated in the caregiving situation."[9]

And she points out that although repaying this debt is, of course, an impossible task, many adult children attempt it nevertheless.[12]

Yet perhaps the importance of filial responsibility lies in another experience, a lesson that many people learn in childhood but that may still leave a lifelong imprint, whatever their adherence to organized religion. Quite possibly, when a person sees an elderly individual with support needs, he or she recalls and feels compelled to heed the biblical commandment, "Honor thy father and mother."

Facing one's own old-age dependency needs. Since reciprocity and/or filial responsibility seem central to explaining why families provide long-term care to their elderly relatives, the intergenerational flow of resources may appear to go only to the older person. However, it is important to note that benefits may also flow back to the provider, an exchange which further underscores the concept of interdependence across the life course.

As mentioned previously, individuals with chronic illnesses or disabilities must come to terms with a diminution of their self-reliance, an acceptance which is extremely difficult for most people to reach. However, just as it is essential for the older person needing support to be able to *give up* some self-reliance and *depend* more on other family members, it is equally essential for those other family members to *accept* the older person's increased need for their support. As Brody points out, "not only must the adult child have the capacity to permit the parent to be dependent, but the parent must have the capacity to be appropriately dependent so as to permit the adult child to be dependable."[13]

Part of the importance to family members obviously lies in the fact that they are the providers of this care. Yet it is important for another, very personal reason as well. It is very difficult for most people to come to terms with having to rely on others for extra-ordinary care. The refusal of older relatives to adjust to their diminished autonomy and to their reliance on others for long-term care needs may make the task even more difficult for all concerned. However, by accepting and dealing with older relatives with extra-ordinary needs, the care-giver can learn to appreciate both the difficulty *and* the necessity of adjusting to diminished autonomy.[14] Thus, care-giving to older family members with chronic problems can have a very positive impact on the personal development of care-givers as well.

Stresses to the Family from Long-Term Care Provision

Long-term care of older family members is similar to other kinds of extra-ordinary care-giving over the life course in that it tests a family's care-giving abilities and requires readjustments in other spheres of family life. Such adjustments often are stressful. In some cases the resulting stresses affect the health and welfare of other family members as well as of the primary provider(s). Generally, however, the closer the relationship to the care-receiver, the greater the strain on the care-giver. Thus spouses, followed by children, tend to be the most stressed.[15]

Stress that results from providing long-term care in family settings falls into five general categories:

- demands on time,
- demands on space,
- demands on financial resources,
- psychological stress, and
- physical stress.

Demands on time. Administering to an affected relative's needs may take hours every day; it may, in fact, use up all free time normally reserved for leisure activities or personal needs. One study of children caring for parents at home found that two-fifths of such children spend as much time at care-giving activities as they would at a full-time job.[16] More recently, a survey of Travelers Insurance Company employees indicated that approximately 20 percent of home office employees aged 30 and over spend an average of 10.2 hours a week providing care to older persons.[17] Still another study, examining three generations of women as care-givers, found that, as middle-aged women grow older, their care-giving responsibilities to their parents increase. Although the sample drawn for the study was fairly small (161), nonrandom, and thus possibly unrepresentative of women across the country, the study found that women in their forties averaged 3 hours per week on care-giving tasks, while those over age 50 averaged more than 15 hours weekly.[18]

In addition to the time needed to perform care-giving tasks, families also must take time to plan the logistics of care-giving (e.g., who takes grandmother to her doctor's appointment; who stops off on the way home from school or work to pick up a special food or prosthetic device). Such activities require daily intergenerational coordination, whether or not the older relative in need of long-term care lives under the same roof with other family members.

Demands on space. In those cases where the chronically ill or disabled individual lives under the same roof, the demands on physical space are obvious. The affected individual often needs his or her own bedroom. Special furniture and prosthetic devices may occupy the living room, kitchen, and bathroom. Medical supplies and special foods may be in the refrigerator or other storage areas. Even when the individual needing long-term care does not live with the family, some family members may experience a constriction of physical space. They may find their daily geographical circuit diminished and may lose the freedom to come and go as they please. For example, they may find travel plans in winter restricted to a distance that would allow them to respond to the increased weather-related needs of the older relative maintaining his or her own residence. Insofar as this is true, not only are *their* lives affected but so, also, are the lives of others in the family.

Demands on financial resources. Spouses frequently bear the brunt of the financial costs of long-term care.[19] For instance, the time a 63-year-old wage-earner spends caring for a disabled spouse often means time out of the labor force and thus lost wages—especially when the care-giving demands are great. And when these demands interfere with the desire and need to remain in the work force until retirement, they can lead to enormous personal financial costs.

Furthermore, many cases of severe disability or illness, such as persons in the advanced stages of Alzheimer's disease, eventually prove to be more than a spouse can handle within the home environment. At this point, many spouses are faced with the necessity of placing the affected individual in a nursing home or some institution. Besides the inordinate emotional stress this decision entails, financial demands are often devastating as life savings are quickly spent for the high costs of services in the first months of institutionalization.

As with demands on space, demands on finances are also intergenerational. Not only does the care-giving spouse face a very uncertain financial future, but that uncertain future can affect any children or grandchildren as well. For one thing, without the counted-on personal financial resources, subsequent financial support of the care-giving spouse is likely to become, at least in part, the family's responsibility. For another thing, "spent down" parents are not in a position to transfer their accumulated assets to their heirs; thus, the children and grandchildren bear the financial loss of inherited wealth, while the affected individual and the care-giving spouse lose the satisfaction of seeing the fruits of their labor transferred to succeeding generations.

Psychological stress. One of the greatest strains shared by family members providing long-term care to chronically ill or disabled older members can be psychological stress. According to Marjorie Cantor, a researcher on the family in an aging society: "Most caregivers protect their families and work, but at considerable personal expense to themselves. It is not surprising, therefore, that the greatest strain experienced by caregivers of dependent elderly is in the emotional area."[20] This psychological strain can take a variety of forms. Indeed, as another researcher notes, "a long litany of mental health symptoms such as depression, anxiety, frustration, helplessness, sleeplessness, lowered morale, and emotional exhaustion are related to restrictions on time and freedom, isolation, conflict from the competing demands of various responsibilities, difficulties in setting priorities, and interference with life-style and social and recreational activities."[21] Thus, not only does psychological stress take on a multiplicity of forms, but these forms are also related to and interact with other types of stress that family members may experience, such as demands on time.

The personification of the individual experiencing psychological stress is the so-called woman in the middle. She represents women who

> are in middle age, in the middle from a generational standpoint, and in the middle in that the demands of their various roles compete for their time and energy. To an extent unprecedented in history, roles as paid workers and as caregiving daughters and daughters-in-law to dependent older people have been added to their traditional roles as wives, homemakers, mothers and grandmothers.*[22]

Often faced with the competing demands of work and family, and then—*within* the family environment—the competing demands of children, spouse, and parents, the woman in the middle is particularly vulnerable to emotional stress. And when the need to provide long-term care to a chronically ill or disabled family member is added to those demands, the resultant stress is greatly intensified. Finally, added to her stress is the frequent denial of personal needs since, faced with competing demands on her time, she is likely to give up her own opportunities for free time, socialization, and recreation.[24]

---

*The woman in the middle is, of course, really a prototype. Coming from a variety of socioeconomic, educational, and ethnic backgrounds, such women may, in fact, be in their thirties or in their sixties. They may be in the second generation of a three-generation family or in the third generation of a four-generation family with a concomitant array of children, grandchildren, parents, and grandparents for whom they fill a care-giving role. What these women "share is a situation produced by major demographic shifts and changes in women's life-styles."[23]

Physical stress. Not surprisingly, research indicates that the woman in the middle and other care-givers also can experience physical health problems as a result of their circumstances. Both the stress of competing demands and the support needs of the ill or disabled older relative require physical stamina. To make matters worse, many of these women are beginning to experience age-related changes, such as a lower energy level and the onset of their own chronic ailments.[25]

The physical strain of long-term care especially affects the spouses of chronically ill or disabled older people. Even if they have not yet experienced any substantial deterioration in health themselves, the physical strain of being the primary care-giver to a chronically ill spouse can be tremendous, often resulting in or contributing to subsequent deterioration in personal health.

DEMOGRAPHIC AND SOCIETAL TRENDS AND FAMILY CARE

The ability and willingness of individual families to handle stresses that may result from providing long-term care vary greatly according to individual circumstances, strength of family ties, and the particular reasons behind a family's decision to provide such care. In general, however, the capacity of families to do so in the future may be significantly diminished by several demographic and societal trends that point to changes in *demand* for care, family structures, and living arrangements.

For example, the nation can expect a sharp increase in the number of elderly requiring long-term care. At the same time, the projected increase in single-parent households and the divorce rate may affect the ability of families to provide care, while the increasing number of women entering the work force may leave women, the traditional care-givers, less available and less willing to provide care on a long-term basis. Also, as increasing numbers of women have fewer or no children, the supply of future family care-givers may also diminish.

Other factors are no doubt at work, but discussion of just the ones listed above will suffice to call attention to potential changes that lie ahead in the intergenerational exchange.

Increasing Numbers of Elderly Requiring Long-Term Care.

Estimates currently indicate that of the 6.6 million elderly persons now requiring some kind of long-term care services, about 5.2 million continue to reside in private homes or in some other type of noninstitutional setting (see chart 3.1).[26] And these numbers are expected to grow.

The increase in the number of elderly requiring long-term care will result primarily from two demographic factors. First, the increased longevity beyond age 65, due to the decrease in the death rate, means that many more people are living to very old age (85 years and older), when they are more likely than ever before in their lives to need long-term care. Second, when the large post-World War II baby boom cohort enters old age during the first half of the twenty-first century, the absolute number of persons in all elderly age groups is projected to increase significantly.[27]

While it is impossible to determine for certain how many elderly will need long-term care in the future, some projections are possible

Chart 3.1
Older Americans in Need of Long-Term Care, 1980–2040

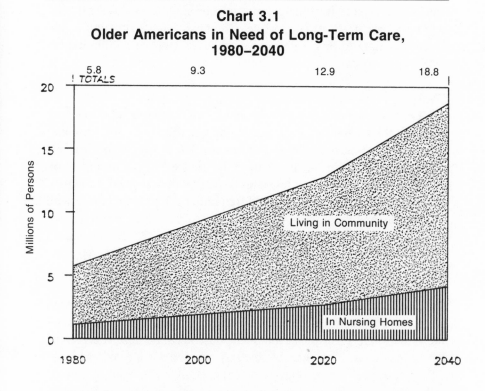

Source: Senate Special Committee on Aging, *Developments in Aging: 1984*, 99th Cong., 1st sess., 28 February 1985, S. Rept. 99-5.

Reprinted from U.S. Senate, *Developments in Aging: 1984*, vol. 1. *A Report of the Special Committee on Aging* (Washington, D.C.: U.S. GPO, 1985).

based on current experience. The need for long-term care is greatest among the very old—with an estimated 62 percent of persons aged 85 and over requiring some kind of long-term care (see chart 2.8).[28] And looking ahead, even if the average age for the onset of disabling conditions from severe arthritis, circulatory problems, etc., is postponed several years, the number of elderly requiring long-term care can be expected to increase. One set of projections suggests that the total elderly long-term care population will increase to more than 9 million by the year 2000, to 12.9 million by 2020, and to nearly 19 million by 2040.

Such an increase in demand for long-term care cannot help but have major implications for care-givers of all descriptions. For example, the large number of Americans reaching very old age may mean that an individual family may have more than one elderly parent requiring long-term care at the same time. Moreover, the woman in the middle, who may herself be entering old age, may also be simultaneously facing the long-term care needs of her spouse. Obviously such a situation would affect the length of time a family would be able and/or willing to provide long-term care.

Changing Family Structures

The traditional two-parent household—with the husband in the labor force and the wife at home—is rapidly being replaced by the combination of one-parent households and households in which both parents are in the labor force. A report from the House Select Committee on Children, Youth, and Families states the case quite succinctly. In 1980, only 47 percent of the nation's children under 6 lived in a family with two parents and the mother not in the work force. That figure is projected to drop to 33 percent by 1990. Simultaneously, we are seeing a growing number of children in poverty. The House Committee notes that while 3.9 million children under 6 lived in poverty in 1980, that figure is projected to reach 4.9 million by 1990.[29]

The increased number of single-parent families created through divorce and through childbirth for unmarried women further complicates the family's care-giving capacity. Such households, because of economic and/or time constraints, may be severely strained when providing long-term care to one or more elderly parents. Similarly, a child of divorce will face some different challenges as well. As one researcher asks, "What will be the relationship between aging fathers and children with whom they had only sporadic contact for many years, and for whom they did not pay regular support?"[30]

Further, for many, divorce will be followed by remarriage. This brings with it an entirely new and often complex kinship structure that will also pose some unexpected challenges to family members' notions of filial loyalty and responsibility.[31] For instance, will one's responsibility lie with blood relatives only, with current in-laws, or with previous in-laws should they require long-term care support? And when remarriage occurs later in life, how will children react when a new step-father or stepmother requires long-term care?

These trends and the figures from the House Committee report cited above suggest a growing demand, if not need, for additional care services to assist families raising children. The figures also give a good indication of the number of families with children that, because both parents are in the labor force or only one parent is present, could be hard-pressed to meet the family's traditional care-giving role over the life course.

Women Working Outside the Home

For several different reasons, women of the baby boom generation have been more career-minded than women of previous generations. How will the women of this cohort, socialized as teenagers and young women to be career-oriented, handle competing demands of employment and family when they reach middle age? If the role of women as primary care-givers is diminished, will men be willing and able to pick up some of the slack and more? How will the employed woman in the middle handle conflicts between "internalized social expectations about filial behavior and the reality demands of her multiple responsibilities to work, self, spouse, and the younger generations"?[32]

Smaller Families

What may be even more broadly felt are the effects of the small *number* of children (currently an average of 1.8 per female of childbearing age) that the baby boom cohort is having. Will these baby bust offspring be able to support their parents' long-term care needs—especially when there is little chance of sharing the burden among several siblings? Demographers Beth Soldo and Kenneth Manton argue that with the death of the spouse, one child—usually a daughter—assumes most of the care-giving tasks, *regardless* of the number of offspring.[33] How great, then, are the pressures on such children when they are faced with the likelihood of more than one parent or parent-in-law requiring long-term care support—perhaps simultaneously or in quick succession?

Furthermore, a large number of baby boomers are not having any children at all. Indeed, Soldo and Manton point out that the real tension point surrounding the long-term care of the baby boom cohort is likely to be the number of *childless* women in the twenty-first century, not the smaller number of offspring the baby boom generation is projected to have.[34] These individuals will not have the option of seeking support from their own children and will have to rely heavily on other relatives or friends. Even more important, many will have *no recourse* but to push for support from public-sector sources.

CONCLUSION

Even the cursory discussion presented in this chapter makes clear the great number and variety of intergenerational transfers that occur as the result of care-giving within the family and the strong preference families have for providing these transfers. We have also tried to indicate demographic and societal trends that will increasingly strain the family's ability and willingness to provide such care. At issue are the traditional values of family-provided care, the quality of life for many care-givers and care-receivers alike, and the costs of providing care.

Examined from the viewpoint of the interdependence of generations, all generations have a common stake in maintaining the family as the primary care-giver across the life course, especially as the family's ability to provide such care is coming increasingly under stress. Clearly, a public policy response will be required to help families continue in their traditional care-giving role. That response should be broad enough to recognize the common stake generations have in preserving that role.

Notes

1. Marjorie H. Cantor, Karen Rosenthal, and Louis Wilker, "Social and Family Relationships of Black Aged Women in New York City" (Paper presented at the Twenty-eighth Annual Scientific Meeting of The Gerontological Society of America, Louisville, Ky., 29 October 1975), 16-18; Cantor and Little, "Aging and Social Care," 757.

2. Louis Harris and Associates, Inc., *The Myth and Reality of Aging in America* (Washington, D.C.: National Council on the Aging, Inc., 1975), 73-74.

3. Ibid., 75.

4. Cantor, Rosenthal, and Wilker, "Black Aged Women"; V.L. Bengston and L. Burton, "Families and Support Systems Among Three Ethnic Groups" (Paper presented at the Thirty-third Annual Scientific Meeting of The Gerontological Society of America, San Diego, Calif., 21-25 November 1980).

5. Thomas J. Espenshade, *Investing in Children: New Estimates of Parental Expenditures* (Washington, D.C.: The Urban Institute Press, 1984), 3.

6. Ibid., 54.

7. "1982 National Long-Term Care Survey," as cited in Senate Special Committee on Aging, *Developments in Aging: 1984*, 189.

8. Amy Horowitz and Lois W. Shindelman, "Reciprocity and Affection: Past Influences on Current Caregiving," *Journal of Gerontological Social Work* 5, no. 3 (n.d.): 6.

9. Ibid., 16-17.

10. Alvin Schorr, ". . . *Thy Father and Thy Mother* . . .": *A Second Look at Filial Responsibility and Family Policy* (Washington, D.C.: Social Security Administration, July 1980), 8-9.

11. Elaine M. Brody, Pauline T. Johnsen, and Mark C. Fulcomer, "What Should Adult Children Do for Elderly Parents? Opinions and Preferences of Three Generations of Women," *Journal of Gerontology* 39, no. 6 (n.d.): 741.

12. Brody, "Parent Care," 26.

13. Ibid., 23.

14. Marjorie H. Cantor, personal conversation, 16 July 1985.

15. Marjorie H. Cantor, "Strain Among Caregivers: A Study of Experiences in the United States," *The Gerontologist* 23 (December 1983): 601.

16. Sandra Newman, et al., *Housing Adjustments of Older People: A Report of Findings from the Second Phase* (Ann Arbor, Mich.: Institute for Social Research, University of Michigan, 1976), 50.

17. Travelers Insurance Company, "Survey Shows Many Travelers Employees Caring for Elderly Relatives or Friends," *News Summary*, 12 December 1985.

18. Abigail M. Lang and Elaine M. Brody, "Characteristics of Middle-Aged Daughters and Help to Their Elderly Mothers," *Journal of Marriage and the Family* (February 1983): 197.

19. Cantor, "Strain Among Caregivers," 600.

20. Ibid., 601.

21. Brody, "Parent Care," 22.

22. Elaine M. Brody, " 'Women in the Middle' and Family Help to Older People," *The Gerontologist* 21 (October 1981): 471.

23. Ibid., 471-472.

24. Brody, "Parent Care," 25.

25. Brody, " 'Women in the Middle,' " 477.

26. Senate Special Committee on Aging, *Development in Aging: 1984*, "1982

National Long-Term Care Survey''; ''1977 National Nursing Home Survey'' and Social Security Administration projections, as cited in Senate Special Committee on Aging, *Developments in Aging: 1984*, 189.

27. Senate Special Committee on Aging, *Developments in Aging: 1984*, 189.

28. Ibid., 190.

29. House Select Committee on Children, Youth, and Families.

30. Gunhild Hagestad, ''The Aging Society as a Context for Family Life,'' *Daedalus* 115 (Winter 1986): 16.

31. Elaine M. Brody, ''The Aging of the Family,'' *Annals of the American Academy of Political and Social Science* 438 (n.d.): 26.

32. Ibid., 25.

33. Soldo and Manton, ''Demographic Challenges for Socioeconomic Planning,'' 238

34. Ibid.

4

The Common Stake In Social Security

JUST as family care-giving illustrates the stake all of us have in *private* intergenerational transfers, Social Security* exemplifies our common stake in intergenerational transfers based on public policy.

The stake that all generations have in Social Security results from

- the widespread preference individuals and families have for nonpersonal means of financial support in old age—that is, for the major responsibility for the financial support of older relatives being placed outside the family;

- the desire individuals and families have for a dignified and stable means of support for the elderly, the disabled, and surviving and financially dependent family members;

- the need for a rational approach that allows individuals to contribute at a relatively low rate over time in exchange for protection for themselves and their families against basic risks such as reduction of income due to retirement, disability, or death of a breadwinner;

---

*The term *Social Security* is used to refer only to the Old-Age and Survivors Insurance (OASI) and Disability Insurance (DI) programs. Medicare, the Hospital Insurance and Supplementary Medical Insurance programs for aged and disabled persons, is sometimes also referred to by others as Social Security. Also, Social Security is sometimes used by others to describe the totality of social insurance programs, such as Social Security and Unemployment Insurance, and public assistance programs, such as the Supplemental Security Income program (SSI), that are designed to protect the economic security of citizens. We use the more restrictive definition of Social Security here because this term is most often used now to describe the retirement, survivors, and disability benefits provided under the Social Security Act.

- the widespread distribution of the benefits and costs of Social Security across all generations;

- the centrality of Social Security as a source of income for the elderly, now and for the foreseeable future; and

- the reality that, despite recent financing problems and smaller rates of return for future cohorts of the elderly, Social Security remains a good deal for persons of all ages.

Our purpose here is not to argue that Social Security or any other intergenerational transfers based on public policies are flawless and should never be changed. Rather, it is simply to point out the common stake existing in such transfers and the importance of recognizing this common stake in terms of understanding who benefits from various policies and the consequences of various policy options.

PREFERENCE FOR NONPERSONAL SUPPORT IN OLD AGE

Notwithstanding the great amount of care-giving that flows to and from parents and children across the life course, the financial independence of adult children is valued both by them and by their parents. Similarly, parents generally do not wish to draw on their children's financial resources, even in advanced old age. They prefer to rely instead on a combination of private savings mechanisms (e.g., private pensions, personal savings) and public programs.

The common stake in Social Security derives, in part, from the desire of individuals and families to place responsibility for the financial support of elderly persons outside the family. A poll conducted by Yankelovich, Skelly, and White, Inc. in 1985 for the American Association of Retired Persons (AARP) testifies to the public's appreciation for the importance of this function. Based on a sample representing the noninstitutionalized population aged 25 and over, 80 percent maintained that providing financial support to parents would be too much of a burden in the absence of Social Security. In the same survey, 88 percent of the respondents opposed phasing out Social Security and substituting reliance on private pensions, in part because of concern that this change would increase the personal responsibility of children for the financial care of older parents.[1]

Happily, the presence of Social Security in combination with private savings has largely freed current and future retirees from relying on their children for financial support, as is evident in another poll conducted for the American Council of Life Insurance and others. Based on a representative sample of Americans aged 50 to 64 in 1984, only 3 percent of respondents employed full or part time (or whose spouses were so employed) expected to receive any income from children or other relatives when they retire, and less than 1 percent expected such support to be their most important source of income in retirement.[2]

DESIRE FOR A DIGNIFIED AND STABLE MEANS OF SUPPORT

In addition to preferring that the major responsibility for income support in old age be placed outside the family, the public also wants a retirement income system that provides a dignified and stable means of support. In fact, preserving the dignity of beneficiaries and ensuring the stability of program financing (and therefore of benefits) are often considered the two most important policy goals of Social Security. Government economist Lawrence Thompson points out that Social Security is "structured first and foremost to produce a system that is financially viable and predictable in the long run despite being controlled by short-run political considerations."[3] The long-run stability of Social Security is reinforced by an understanding that it involves a compact between generations and between government and the citizenry. And as Brandeis economist James Schulz observes, living "with dignity and trust that there will be a future is at the heart of the aspirations and values" of many people, and Social Security responds to these concerns.[4] The great importance Congress and the people place on preserving dignity helps explain the high value attached both to the receipt of benefits as a matter of right and to social adequacy.

The Common Stake in Benefits as a Matter of Right

Americans simply do not like means-tested programs. Welfare programs are considered demeaning. Further, as Wilbur Cohen points out, programs for poor people become poor programs.[5]

The widespread support for Social Security relates to its contributory nature. Through payroll tax contributions, workers and their employers earn the right for themselves and their families to receive benefits when covered risks actualize. These contributions enhance the sense of dignity citizens have when receiving Social Security.[6]

The Common Stake in Social Adequacy

The concern for dignity similarly highlights the importance of social

71

adequacy—the principle that program benefits should be sufficient to meet the basic needs of persons the program is designed to protect. However, this goal often conflicts with the goal of individual equity— the principle that persons who pay into a system should receive a return from that system directly proportionate to their contributions (or contributions made on their behalf).

Much misunderstanding about Social Security derives from a lack of understanding both of the public stake in social adequacy and of the roles the principles of adequacy and individual equity play in social insurance programs—programs in which the prior contribution of workers and/or their employers establishes the right to government benefits. Unlike private insurance programs, social insurance programs hold social adequacy as a major goal—some would, in fact, call it the dominant goal. In 1938, Reinhard Hohaus, an actuary and executive with the Metropolitan Life Insurance Company, wrote that, whereas private insurance is designed to meet the individual's need for protection against various risks, social insurance is designed to meet society's need to provide a floor of protection for citizens against critical social hazards. Payments to persons experiencing these risks

> must be met in one form or another anyway, and social insurance endeavors to organize the budgeting therefore and dispensing thereof through systematic governmental processes. Hence, *just as considerations of equity of benefits form a natural and vital part of operating private insurance, so should considerations of adequacy control the pattern of social insurance benefits.* [Emphasis added] Likewise, as private insurance would collapse if it stressed considerations of adequacy more than those of equity, so will social insurance fail to remain undisturbed if considerations of equity are allowed to predominate over those of adequacy.[7]

Robert Myers, chief actuary of Social Security from 1947 to 1970 and most recently executive director of the National Commission on Social Security Reform, also points out that the real reason for having social insurance programs is "that social benefits on a social-adequacy basis can only in this way be provided to a large sector of the population."[8]

The Social Security benefit structure actually represents a compromise between the two goals of social adequacy and individual equity. The provision of auxiliary benefits to certain family members, the weighted benefit formula which provides proportionately larger benefits to lower-income workers (and their families), and the cost-of-living adjustment (COLA) provision all reflect the principle of adequacy. But concern for individual equity is reflected as well in that benefits are also earnings-related: higher wages and payroll tax contributions generally yield larger benefit amounts.[9] Failure to understand the centrality of social adequacy engenders false criticism of Social Security as being a "welfare program." Also, although the proportionately smaller benefits that higher-income earners will receive are sometimes cited in arguments that young workers will not receive a "fair rate of return" on their benefits, this type of argument has two real shortcomings. First, it overlooks the importance of judging the fairness of the program in terms of the treatment of birth cohorts as a whole rather than as particular subgroups. Second, it also overlooks the fact that some compromise of the principle of individual equity is the price that must be paid in a system that also values social adequacy.

Social Security as a Compact

Social Security is often referred to as a compact between citizens and the government, and it is often considered an intergenerational compact as well. These perspectives help explain why pay-as-you-go financing is generally sufficient to guarantee the continuity and stability of the program.

As Myers points out, while Social Security involves a statutory right, the specific provisions can be changed by the legislature or other responsible authority.[10] Payroll tax contributions, however, increase both the contractual nature of the relationship between government and the citizenry and the political necessity for government to maintain the program's continuity as well as promised benefits. To a large degree, this assures the program's existence for each birth cohort. Further, as Thompson states, contributory financing provides an "institutional check against the political temptation to overpromise" by linking benefit liberalizations "directly to increases in a highly visible tax."[11]

Viewed as a compact between generations, Social Security is seen to involve present generations of workers paying taxes to support current beneficiaries, with the understanding that future workers will do the same for them when the risks they are being protected against actualize.

Thus, the taxing power of the government and the notion of an intergenerational compact guarantee the continuity of Social Security. According to J. Douglas Brown, there is an implied covenant in Social Security, arising from a deeply embedded sense of mutual responsibility in civilization, that underlies the "fundamental obligation of the government and the citizens of one time and the government and the citizens of another time to maintain a contributory social insurance system."[12]

NEED FOR A RATIONAL APPROACH TO PROTECTING AGAINST BASIC RISKS

Individuals and families need protection against risks to which everybody is subject: loss of income due to retirement, disability, or death of a wage earner. For this reason, all of us have a stake in social insurance. In exchange for making contributions at a relatively low rate over time, Social Security provides substantial protection against large and sudden costs that can arise from the occurrence of such risks and that would otherwise probably overwhelm most individuals and families.

Further, these risks are compounded by a great deal of uncertainty. For example, in terms of planning for retirement, Schulz points out that individuals do not know 1) the number of years they or their survivors will live, 2) whether unemployment or poor health will reduce their employability, 3) when they will retire, 4) the future rate of inflation for which they must plan during their retirement,[13] or 5) the preretirement standard of living that they will try to maintain throughout their retirement.

In the face of so much uncertainty, individuals and families obviously have a stake in protecting themselves against economic insecurity. And again, the social insurance mechanism (private pensions and private insurance to a more limited degree) is a response to this need. Through COLAs, for instance, Social Security substantially reduces the risk to beneficiaries of inflation eroding their economic welfare.

Additionally, individuals and families have a stake in assuring that other members of society are also protected against basic risks, since without such protection, some costs associated with retirement, disability, or death of a breadwinner would, of necessity, be borne through public welfare expenditures. Consequently, Social Security also protects against the shortsighted decisions of some (not to protect against basic risks), which later may result in public costs to others.

The common stake in Social Security, then, is related to the need for a rational mechanism both to protect against economic insecurity in the face of uncertainty and, to a lesser degree, to protect against the potentially shortsighted decisions of others. Social Security meets the first need through the use of insurance principles, including the pooling of risks and the use of actuarial principles to estimate benefits and costs.[14] It meets the second need through the fact that it is—and must be—compulsory.[15] If voluntary, persons of low risk would tend to opt out, leaving a disproportionate number of high-risk people in the insurance pool and thereby undermining the financing of the program. And, as has been pointed out, some of those who would choose not to participate in the program would later be in need of assistance that would require public expenditures.[16] In the event of a major calamity, this group could be enormous. Further, unlike private insurance, the Social Security program does not turn away prospective participants on the ground that they are "bad risks." By assuring an insurance pool with a mix of good and bad risks, the compulsory aspect of the program enables the program to accept poor risks. Thus, the public has an obvious stake in the compulsory nature of Social Security.

THE WIDESPREAD DISTRIBUTION
OF BENEFITS AND COSTS

The common stake in Social Security is also a result of the widespread distribution of program benefits and costs among persons of all ages. To understand this, it is important to take both a static and a long-term view of how such benefits and costs are distributed. From the static view, which emphasizes the *direct* benefits and costs of the program *at one point in time*, the direct benefits go largely (about 85 percent), but not exclusively, to retired workers, spouses of retired workers, and widows and widowers aged 60 and over. In contrast, from the long-term view, which examines the *direct* and *indirect* benefits of Social Security *over time*, many indirect benefits clearly accrue primarily to the young, while others result in general improvements in the quality of American life.

Direct Benefits and Costs: The Static Perspective
Benefits: the cross-sectional perspective. In terms of direct benefits, Social Security protects nearly every American against loss of income due to retirement, disability, or death of a wage earner. As already noted, the payroll tax contributions workers (and their employers) make establish the rights individuals and their families have to benefits.

Each month about 37 million persons receive Social Security cash benefits. Most are retired workers and their spouses (about 26 million persons). Some 4.7 million persons are the survivors (mostly widows), 60 and over, of retired workers. Many, such as the 3 million disabled workers and their spouses, are not elderly. In fact, about 3.3 million

75

children, mostly the young dependents of deceased and disabled workers, receive Social Security benefits each month, as do about 370,000 surviving spouses (mostly widows under 60) who are caring for young children.[17]

Monthly benefits under Social Security vary, depending on previous earnings, size of family, and age at initial receipt of benefits. Data in table 4.1 indicate the value of benefits to individuals and families. In looking at these benefits, one should keep in mind that Social Security is not intended to be the only source of income for beneficiaries.

It is also important to keep in mind that the automatic COLA provides very substantial protection to beneficiaries against the inflation-based erosion of benefits, even though the certainty of the COLA has been slightly compromised in the past few years.* This feature of the law—virtually unmatched by private pensions—has very direct benefit to all.

Costs: the cross-sectional perspective. The direct costs at any one point in time are fairly clear. Table 4.2 presents the payroll tax rates and maximum amount of earnings (the "Contribution and Benefit Base") on which these taxes are levied for the combined Old-Age and Survivors Insurance and Disability Insurance (OASDI) trust funds. In 1986, employees and their employers will each make payroll tax contribu-

---

*Beginning with the July 1975 check to beneficiaries, the 1972 amendments to the Social Security Act provided for automatic cost-of-living adjustments to go into effect whenever the yearly increase in inflation was 3.0 percent or more, as measured by the increase in the average CPI from the first quarter of the previous year in which benefit adjustments had been made through the first quarter of the current year. The 1983 amendments to the Social Security Act delayed the COLA by six months and provided for all future COLAs to be reflected in the January checks rather than six months earlier in the previous July checks. The permanent six-month delay represents a benefit reduction for all current and future beneficiaries of approximately 2 percent. Also, the measuring periods are now based on the increase in the CPI from the third quarter of the previous year in which a COLA has been made through the third quarter of the current year. Finally, the 1983 amendments provided that, beginning in 1985, if the combined trust fund ratio is extremely low (defined roughly as less than needed to meet two months of benefit payments prior to 1989 and about two and one-half months of payments thereafter), the COLA will be based on the lesser of the increases in prices or in wages until the trust funds return to a safer level. Should it ever be necessary to give a smaller COLA based on changes in average wages rather than prices, the 1983 amendments also provide for "catch-up" increases when the combined trust funds have sufficient assets to meet roughly four months of anticipated outgo. More recently, the idea of "skipping" the COLA (or reducing it) has been advanced as part of a package directed at dealing with the federal budget deficit.

Table 4.1
Estimated Average and Maximum Social Security Benefits in January 1986

Type of Beneficiary	Average Dollar Benefits Per Month	Maximum Dollar Benefits Per Month
All Retired Workers	478	760
Worker Retiring at Age 65	576	760
Aged Couple (Spouse Did Not Work)	812	1140
Surviving Aged Spouse	431	760
Disabled Worker	483	960
Disabled Worker and Family	899	1440
Young Surviving Family	1017	1727

[a] These maximum benefits apply to persons first eligible in January 1986.

Source: Social Security Administration.

tions into the combined OASDI trust funds of 5.7 percent on earnings through $42,000. The self-employed will make contributions into the combined OASDI trust funds of 11.4 percent on earnings through $42,000, which will be partially offset by a tax credit on self-employment income up to the maximum taxable earnings base. When the contributions into Medicare's Hospital Insurance Trust Fund are included—1.45 percent for wage earners and 2.9 percent for the self-employed (again with a partial tax credit offset)—the maximum tax paid into the combined OASDI trust funds will be $3,003 by wage earners and $5,166 for the self-employed (a net tax rate of 12.3 percent after adjusting for the receipt of tax credits).[18]

For most workers, however, the actual payroll tax contributions are considerably less. A worker earning average wages (about $16,595) in 1985[19] would have made payroll tax contributions into the combined OASDI trust funds of approximately $946, with his or her employer paying the same amount.* (Approximately $241 would have been paid into Medicare's Hospital Insurance Trust Fund, which would also have been matched by the employer's contribution.)

About 125 million workers and their employers will make payroll tax contributions into the combined OASDI trust funds in 1986. The total will amount to about $209 billion.[20] When looked at cross-sectionally—that is, at one point in time—current workers appear to

---

*Most studies show that workers in the long run pay the employer's portion of the payroll tax contribution as well as the employee's portion.

Table 4.2
Contribution and Benefit Base and Contribution Rate

| | | Contribution rates (percent) | | | | | |
| | | Employees and employers, each | | | Self-employed | | |
Calendar years	Contribution and benefit base	OASDI	OASI	DI	OASDI	OASI	DI
1937–49	$3,000	1.000	1.000	—	—	—	—
1950	3,000	1.500	1.500	—	—	—	—
1951–53	3,600	1.500	1.500	—	2.2500	2.2500	—
1954	3,600	2.000	2.000	—	3.0000	3.0000	—
1955–56	4,200	2.000	2.000	—	3.0000	3.0000	—
1957–58	4,200	2.250	2.000	0.250	3.3750	3.0000	0.3750
1959	4,800	2.500	2.250	.250	3.7500	3.3750	.3750
1960–61	4,800	3.000	2.750	.250	4.5000	4.1250	.3750
1962	4,800	3.125	2.875	.250	4.7000	4.3250	.3750
1963–65	4,800	3.625	3.375	.250	5.4000	5.0250	.3750
1966	6,600	3.850	3.500	.350	5.8000	5.2750	.5250
1967	6,600	3.900	3.550	.350	5.9000	5.3750	.5250
1968	7,800	3.800	3.325	.475	5.8000	5.0875	.7125
1969	7,800	4.200	3.725	.475	6.3000	5.5875	.7125
1970	7,800	4.200	3.650	.550	6.3000	5.4750	.8250
1971	7,800	4.600	4.050	.550	6.9000	6.0750	.8250
1972	9,000	4.600	4.050	.550	6.9000	6.0750	.8250
1973	10,800	4.850	4.300	.550	7.0000	6.2050	.7950
1974	13,200	4.950	4.375	.575	7.0000	6.1850	.8150
1975	14,100	4.950	4.375	.575	7.0000	6.1850	.8150
1976	15,300	4.950	4.375	.575	7.0000	6.1850	.8150
1977	16,500	4.950	4.375	.575	7.0000	6.1850	.8150
1978	17,700	5.050	4.275	.775	7.1000	6.0100	1.0900
1979	22,900	5.080	4.330	.750	7.0500	6.0100	1.0400
1980	25,900	5.080	4.520	.560	7.0500	6.2725	.7775
1981	29,700	5.350	4.700	.650	8.0000	7.0250	.9750
1982	32,400	5.400	4.575	.825	8.0500	6.8125	1.2375
1983	35,700	5.400	4.775	.625	8.0500	7.1125	.9375
1984[1]	37,800	5.700	5.200	.500	11.4000	10.4000	1.0000
1985[1]	39,600	5.700	5.200	.500	11.4000	10.4000	1.0000
1986[1]	42,000	5.700	5.200	.500	11.4000	10.4000	1.0000
Rates scheduled in present law:							
1987[1]	(²)	5.700	5.200	.500	11.4000	10.4000	1.0000
1988–89[1]	(²)	6.060	5.530	.530	12.1200	11.0600	1.0600
1990–99	(²)	6.200	5.600	.600	12.4000	11.2000	1.2000
2000 and later	(²)	6.200	5.490	.710	12.4000	10.9800	1.4200

[1]In 1984 only, an immediate tax credit of 0.3 percent of covered wages was allowed against the OASDI contributions paid by employees, resulting in an effective contribution rate of 5.4 percent (as compared to the employer rate of 5.7 percent). Similar credits of 2.7 percent, 2.3 percent, and 2.0 percent are allowed against the combined OASDI and HI contributions on net earnings from self-employment in 1984, 1985, and 1986–89, respectively.

²Subject to automatic adjustment.

Source: Board of Trustees, Federal Old-Age and Survivors Insurance and Disability Trust Funds, *1985 Annual Report of the Board of Trustees of the Federal Old-Age and Survivors Insurance and Disability Insurance Trust Funds* (Washington, D.C.: U.S. GPO, 1985).

bear the cost of Social Security benefits. There is some truth in this view because, for the most part, worker contributions in any given year are used primarily* to pay for benefits received during that year. However, two points should be noted. First, beginning in 1984, up to 50 percent of Social Security benefits have been treated as taxable for higher-income beneficiaries with the resultant revenue being transferred into the combined OASDI trust funds (about $4.1 billion in 1986). Second, some elderly are working and therefore still making payroll tax contributions. Consequently, even from a cross-sectional point of view, some beneficiaries do make tax payments to Social Security.

Direct and Indirect Benefits and Costs: The Long-Term Perspective
Benefits: the longitudinal perspective. Viewing Social Security over time and in terms of both direct and indirect benefits results in a very different understanding of who benefits. To begin with, it must be recognized that Social Security is an institution with a 50-year history and a strong and financially viable future.[21] This does not suggest that there never have been nor ever will be problems, or that the program will not change over time; note, for instance, the recent financing problems of the Social Security cash programs, which were resolved in 1983. Social Security, however, is so fundamental to our society that no president and no Congress would ever allow the program to fail to meet its obligations. And when it is clearly understood that Social Security is an institution that will continue through time, it is easy to see that, in the long run, current workers will be the direct beneficiaries.

The long-run perspective is also necessary to understand how Social Security introduces a critical element of stability into retirement plans. The Social Security benefit formula guarantees that a constant proportion of prior earnings will be replaced for workers at different earning levels. For younger workers, this means that, even before benefits are first received, their value is kept up-to-date with rising wages and increases in the standard of living.

In fact, the retirement benefits for today's younger workers will be considerably larger (on average)—that is, they will have greater purchasing power—than those of today's retirees (even though the rate of

---

*Note that beginning in the late 1980s, very substantial surpluses will begin to build up in the trust funds; as a result, for many years, significant portions of workers' payroll taxes will also contribute to these surpluses, which will later be used to help finance the retirement benefits of the baby boomers.

return on their Social Security "investment" will generally be smaller).*
The growth of wages over their lives will be translated by the benefit
formula into larger benefits. (Of course, their tax contributions will have
been greater, too.) Using modest assumptions about the growth of the
economy (an average of about 2 percent real growth per year over the
next 75 years), Social Security's actuaries project that, whereas a worker
who earned average wages throughout his life and retired at age 65 in
1985 would receive $548 a month, a similar worker retiring at age 65
in 2000 would receive $659, and one retiring at age 65 in 2015 would
receive $761 (see table 4.3).

These figures are in inflation-adjusted dollars. The actual dollar
amounts retired workers will receive in the future will be much larger,
of course. For instance, it is projected that a worker retiring at age 65
in 2030 who has earned average wages during all his working years
will receive a *monthly* Social Security benefit of about $5,294! In 1985
dollars, however, this amount will actually be worth about $873. Con-
sequently, it is more informative to use inflation-adjusted dollars. To
use unadjusted dollars would be as misleading as those advertisements
that tell young people they will be millionaires by the time they reach
retirement age if only they put $2,000 a year into IRAs.

Not only will average retirement benefits of future retired workers
be larger, but retirees of the future can generally expect to receive
benefits for a longer period of time than previous cohorts of retirees.
In 1940, when Social Security first paid benefits, life expectancy for
men at age 65 was 11.9 years and for women, 13.4 years. Life expectancy at age 65 in 1985 is estimated to have increased to 14.7 and 19.1
years, respectively, and for those reaching age 65 in 2010, life expec-

---

*While it is true that the purchasing power of Social Security for future beneficiaries
will, on average, be greater, it is also true that the rate of return on younger workers'
Social Security investment will generally be lower than that of current retirees. This
is mainly because, in the early years of Social Security, benefits were paid to persons who made relatively small contributions into the system. Most pension
programs—both public and private—provide special benefits in their start-up phase
to workers nearing retirement. As Robert Ball writes, "No one would think of
establishing a (private) pension plan . . . that did nothing for people who were nearing retirement age at the time it was set up." Private employers "always give past
service credits" under such circumstances.[22] That is similar to what Social Security
did. So it is not surprising that the rate of return for workers retiring early in the
history of the program was considerably higher than that anticipated for future retirees.
The important point for young workers is that Social Security provides a reasonable
rate of return to them and, at the same time, serves many other important functions—
including providing guarantees and protection (e.g., against inflation) generally
unavailable elsewhere.

Table 4.3
Projected Initial Benefits for Persons First Receiving Retirement Benefits at Age 65 (in 1985 dollars)

Year Reaching Age 65	Monthly Benefits for Workers Earning Average Wages[a]	Maximum Monthly Benefits for High-Income Workers[b]
1985	548	717
2000	659	950
2015	761	1190
2030	873	1371

[a] For hypothetical worker with average wages throughout worklife.
[b] For hypothetical worker with maximum taxable earnings throughout worklife.

Source: Social Security Administration (projected benefits based on Alternative IIB Intermediate Assumptions used in the 1985 Trustees Report adjusted to reflect the actual figure for the 1984 average wage).

tancy at age 65 is projected to be 16.1 years for men and 21.1 years for women.[23] Recent and anticipated increases in life expectancy imply that current and future cohorts of workers reaching normal retirement ages (currently 65, 66 for those attaining that age in 2009, and 67 for those attaining it in 2027) will, on average, receive Social Security benefits for a longer period of time after the normal retirement age than those cohorts who reached age 65 early in the life of the program. (On the other hand, because the age of eligibility for full retirement benefits is scheduled to increase in two gradual steps from 65 to 66 and then from 66 to 67 from 2000 through 2027, workers retiring at the age of eligibility for full benefits in 2010 and 2030 will generally receive benefits for a shorter period of time than workers retiring at age 65 in 1985.)

Turning now from the direct to the indirect benefits of Social Security, we can see that the indirect benefits that are going to families, especially young ones, are numerous. One way of identifying some of them is to consider the implications for younger families and individuals if Social Security ceased to exist.

About 60 percent of all aged households receiving retirement income depend on Social Security for at least half their incomes.[24] If Social Security did not exist (and if other financial resources and retirement timing remained the same), poverty rates among the elderly would increase from 14 percent to about 50 percent. Millions more would suffer very significant reductions in their standards of living. Of course, over the long run, private mechanisms (e.g., savings and private pensions)

81

and welfare programs would expand somewhat, with taxpayers having to pick up the additional cost for the latter. Even so, without significant social insurance protection, the elderly would be far more vulnerable to economic insecurity (as, unfortunately, is true for children today).

Clearly, the elderly and other program beneficiaries would have to turn somewhere for help. But to whom? Family members would also have to do much more in the form of direct support. Contrary to popular belief, families already provide considerable personal care to members with significant functional limitations, such as the frail elderly, who often require assistance with routine activities like dressing and shopping (see chap. 3). In terms of direct financial assistance, however, families could only do so much. Younger and middle-aged families with young children would probably be caught between the need to pay household expenses, including the children's education, and the need to provide support to their parents.

Social Security has enabled many older persons to choose whether to live with their children or by themselves. Most elderly choose to live independently but, when possible, relatively close to their children. William Birdsall, a professor at the University of Michigan, notes that census data confirm the view that the "existence of Social Security has reduced private transfers in the form of shared living"; the data show that between 1940 and 1970—a period in which Social Security coverage and benefits greatly increased—the rate at which women aged 70 through 74 lived in the households of others (mostly relatives not counting spouses) dropped from 34 percent to 16 percent.[25] Plainly, without Social Security, some elderly and their children who prefer to maintain independent households would not be able to do so.

Perhaps the key point is that, either way, the young help to a large extent to defray the costs of the elderly. The difference is that Social Security enables each of us (beginning when we are young) to pay out at relatively low and predictable rates over a long period of time, thereby generally enabling us to avoid much larger and financially disruptive expenses at fairly unpredictable points in the life course.

Plainly, by protecting older family members against loss of income due to retirement, Social Security benefits family members of all ages. But even more indirect benefits accrue primarily to the young. According to data provided by the Department of Housing and Urban Development, 11 percent of the elderly living in low-income housing in 1977, and 21 percent in the case of elderly blacks, had one or more children under 18 living in their households.[26] Additionally, Census Bureau data indicate that in 1982 about 4.9 million children under 18 resided in a home where someone received Social Security (or railroad retirement) benefits.[27] While most of these children were the young "dependents" of deceased or disabled workers, a significant number were in homes in which elderly persons also lived. In all likelihood, these children "ate out of the same pot" as the resident elderly persons, and probably there was also considerable commingling of the financial resources that flow to all generations in these households. Consequently, such multigenerational households provide an excellent example of how nonelderly persons benefit indirectly from Social Security.

There are other examples of indirect benefits as well. For one thing, Social Security opens up employment opportunities for younger workers by encouraging older ones to retire in exchange for a pension. For another, without Social Security, welfare costs would be much greater because families simply could not replace most of the protections these programs provide.

Finally, it is important to appreciate that private insurance and social insurance alike have tangible worth, even if the risks being protected against are not realized. Thus, a homeowner renews fire insurance even though his or her house did not burn down in the previous year. Moreover, it is estimated that for a worker with a nonworking spouse and two children under age 6, Social Security is the equivalent of a life insurance policy worth approximately $184,000 in 1985 and a disability insurance policy of similar worth.[28] Comparable protection through private insurance could be fairly costly. For example, one insurance company estimates that the yearly premium for a 35-year-old, nonsmoking man would be $801 for a $184,000 30-year decreasing term life insurance policy.* Thus, disability and survivors protection also have very real value to covered workers and their families.

Costs: the longitudinal perspective. Again, the question arises, who pays for Social Security? Earlier we pointed out that from a cross-sectional perspective—at one point in time—it appears that Social Security benefits accrue primarily to the old and the costs primarily to the young. But this is only so if current workers are receiving nothing in return for their payroll tax contributions. As has been shown, even before direct benefits are paid out, current workers receive very significant indirect

---

*Note that the comparison between Social Security survivors protection and private life insurance benefits is, of necessity, very rough. For one thing, Social Security survivors benefits are indexed to protect against inflation, whereas private life insurance benefits are not; and for another, the amount of survivors benefits under Social Security will generally vary according to factors such as the number of young children and their ages whereas life insurance benefits generally do not.

benefits from the program. Equally important, their payroll tax contributions are earning the right to benefits for themselves and their families. Over time, nearly all will be direct beneficiaries of the program. Therefore, while the system may operate on a largely pay-as-you-go basis, it is important to recognize that each group of beneficiaries has contributed to its members' benefits—except, of course, the early cohorts of beneficiaries, who—as is also true of the early cohorts in private pension plans—clearly benefited from the program's initial start-up.

General Social Benefits

Can it be concluded from this overview of direct and indirect benefits of Social Security that the young do better than the old? Or that the old do better than the young? In reality, it is quite difficult—and probably irrelevant—to determine who does best. The point is that *Social Security is an intergenerational transfer from which all benefit.*

Social Security has value to the nation beyond the benefits it provides: it improves the quality of life for all. By providing a mechanism that enables families and individuals to protect themselves against some major financial risks, this program stabilizes family life and the society.

Moreover, while relieving younger family members of some responsibility for meeting age-related needs has clear financial value, it has human value as well. *It prevents strain in family relations that can accompany the provision of financial assistance to older (or disabled or surviving) family members. It also enables millions of people to maintain financial independence and dignity through the receipt of benefits they have earned. And it is simply impossible to measure the value of self-respect for the elderly, the disabled, and the survivors of deceased workers.*[29]

Finally, because Social Security helps stabilize and hold the nation together with all generations sharing in its costs and benefits, *all generations have a common stake in this program.*

CENTRALITY OF SOCIAL SECURITY AS A SOURCE OF RETIREMENT INCOME

The common stake in Social Security also grows out of its centrality as a source of retirement income, now and for the foreseeable future. Why is this so? Before we answer, two things should be kept in mind. First, the major source of data on the income of the elderly, the Current Population Surveys (CPS), somewhat overstates the importance of Social Security (see chap. 2, n. 7). Second, while this section focuses on sources of cash income in old age, the economic well-being of the elderly is also affected by in-kind transfers (both private and governmental) and the use of consumer durables (e.g., homes) acquired over a lifetime, as well as by the levels of taxation to which the elderly are subject.[30]

Social Security: The Heart of the Nation's Retirement System

Social Security was never intended to be the only source of income in retirement. It is just the building block for the economic well-being of individuals and their families in retirement, to be supplemented by other pension income, personal savings, and possibly part- or full-time employment. As Alicia Munnell, senior vice-president of the Federal Reserve Bank of Boston, notes in congressional testimony:

> The heart of the nation's retirement system is the social security program which covers nearly the entire working population. . . . Because coverage is universal, workers can move from job to job and continue to build up benefits that keep pace with the growth of their earnings. After retirement, a progressive benefit formula provides relatively larger benefits to lower paid workers and annual cost-of-living adjustments ensure that benefits keep pace with prices. Without such adjustments a retiree's economic welfare depends entirely on the vagaries of the economy—a situation that undermines the establishment of a rational retirement system. This universal, fully indexed pension plan now provides benefits to over 90 percent of the elderly.[31]

Data from the Census Bureau's CPS and from the 1982 New Beneficiary System (NBS) of the Social Security Administration show to what extent Social Security figures as a source of income to the elderly. The sample used for the CPS represents noninstitutionalized, unmarried elderly persons or couples with at least one member aged 65 or over. The sample used for the NBS represents workers (and their spouses) who first received Social Security benefits at age 62 or older during the 12-month period from mid-1980 to mid-1981. The interviews occurred from October through December 1982.

Taken together, the data presented in table 4.4 and the trend data presented in charts 4.1 and 4.2 highlight both the importance of Social Security as a source of income to the elderly and to the newly retired (particularly to those who are not married), and the declining significance

85

of earnings. For example, these data indicate that about 90 percent of all elderly households receive Social Security benefits and that Social Security provides about 35 percent of the total income going to all married elderly couples and 45 percent of the total income going to all unmarried elderly persons. In the case of earnings, the reduced significance of this source of income is tied to the decline in labor force participation among older men. For example, the labor force participation of men aged 65 and over declined from about 48 percent in 1947 to about 16 percent in 1985.[32]

Table 4.4
Percent of Total Income from Specific Sources, New Beneficiaries and Population 65 + , 1982

Source of Income	New Beneficiaries[a]		Population 65 and Over	
	Percent Receiving	Percent of Total Income	Percent Receiving	Percent of Total Income[b]
Married Couples				
Social Security	98	34	92	35
Pensions	56	18	49	15
Public	21	n.a.	18	8
Private	38	n.a.	33	7
Assets	84	23	77	24
Earnings	44	22	36	23
Other	16	3	21	1
Unmarried Individuals				
Social Security	97	41	89	45
Pensions	42	18	26	14
Public	16	n.a.	12	8
Private	27	n.a.	15	5
Assets	69	20	61	27
Earnings	27	15	12	10
Other	15	6	24	4

[a]New beneficiaries consist of a sample of 18,599 noninstitutionalized persons who first entered payment status between mid-1980 and mid-1981 and were interviewed from October through December 1982.

[b]The total amount of income received from Social Security and public and private pensions is understated because amounts are excluded for persons receiving both Social Security and railroad retirement benefits and persons receiving both government and private pensions.

Source: Susan Grad, *Income of the Population 55 and Over, 1982* (Social Security Administration, 1984), tables 1, 44, and 45, pp. 2-3 and 78-79; and Linda Drazga Maxfield and Virginia P. Reno, "Distribution of Income Sources of Recent Retirees: Findings from the New Beneficiaries Survey," *Social Security Bulletin* 48, no. 1 (January 1985), tables 1-3, pp. 9-10.

Reprinted from testimony of Alicia H. Munnell, "Retirement Income Security in the United States," presented before the House Subcommittee on Social Security and Subcommittee on Oversight of the Committee on Ways and Means, 18 July 1985.

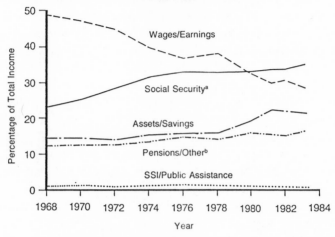

Chart 4.1
Income Shares by Source of Income
Families with Head Aged 65 +
1968–83

Wages/Earnings

Social Security[a]

Assets/Savings

Pensions/Other[b]

SSI/Public Assistance

Percentage of Total Income

Year

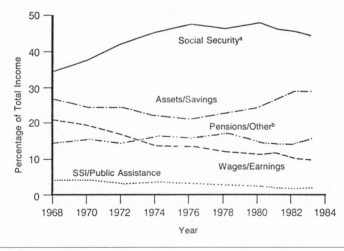

Chart 4.2
Income Shares by Source of Income
Unrelated Individuals 65 +
1968–83

Social Security[a]

Assets/Savings

Pensions/Other[b]

Wages/Earnings

SSI/Public Assistance

Percentage of Total Income

Year

[a]Includes Social Security and railroad retirement.
[b]Includes veterans' payments, unemployment, workers compensation, annuities and alimony.
Source: Bureau of the Census, *Current Population Surveys*, 1969–83, unpublished data.

87

The data presented in charts 4.1 and 4.2 also highlight the modest growth in the importance of private pensions, public-employee pensions, and assets as sources of income. Receipt of private and public-employee pension income has increased substantially since the early 1960s. From 1968 through 1983, however, the total contribution of these sources (as a percent of the aggregate income of the elderly) remained about the same, showing very limited increases during this period. Even so, the number of beneficiaries of private and public-employee pensions increased from 1.7 million in 1960[33] to 10.9 million in 1983, and the number of workers covered by private pensions increased from about 4 million in 1940 to 10 million in 1950, 20 million in 1960,[34] and 39.1 million in 1983—about 56 percent[35] of nonagricultural workers. Nevertheless, this does not begin to approach the universality of Social Security, which covers 125 million workers and provides monthly benefits to 37 million persons. Nor do private and public-employee pensions provide the stability of benefits. Vesting rules, limited portability, inability to index for inflation, and the possibility of plan terminations all potentially reduce the value and certainty of benefits for covered workers and beneficiaries.

While Social Security plainly is pivotal in the retirement income system, the vast majority of aged households receive income from at least one other source (see table 4.4). Next to Social Security, assets* have become the most important source of retirement income. Such income is, however, distributed very unevenly among the elderly, with higher-income households more likely to receive substantial amounts from assets, private and public-employee pensions, or earnings. Further, lower-income elderly households and the very old generally receive a greater proportion of their income from Social Security than do other elderly households (see table 4.5). In fact, data from the NBS indicate that Social Security "remains the main component of income for retirees up through the middle of the income distribution."[36] These data also indicate that while recent retirees (aged 62 and over) usually have other income from pensions or assets, the monthly amount from these sources is often small. Up through the 60th percentile of the income distribution for couples and the 80th percentile for unmarried persons, "average income from social security is larger than the combined average income from pensions and assets."[37]

---

*Given the tendency to underreport assets income, it is probable that the CPS and NBS data somewhat understate the importance of assets (which include interest, dividend, rent, royalty, and trust incomes).

Table 4.5
Percent of Total Income from Specified Sources,
Units Aged 65 and Over, by Age and Income, 1982

Source of Income[a]	All Units[b]	Age			
		65–67	68–72	73–79	80 and Older
Social Security	39	28	38	44	48
Pensions	14	15	15	14	11
Public	8	8	8	8	7
Private	6	7	7	6	4
Assets	25	18	24	30	31
Earnings	18	35	19	9	4
Other	3	3	3	2	4

Source of Income	All Units	Income			
		Under $5,000	$5,000– 9,999	$10,000– 19,999	$20,000 or More
Social Security	39	80	69	46	19
Pensions	14	2	8	16	16
Public	8	1	4	8	9
Private	6	1	4	8	7
Assets	25	4	12	21	36
Earnings	18	0	5	14	27
Other	3	13	5	2	1

[a]The total amount of income received from Social Security and public and private pensions is understated because amounts are excluded for persons receiving both Social Security and railroad retirement benefits and persons receiving both government and private pensions.

[b]Units are married couples and unmarried individuals.

Source: Susan Grad, *Income of the Population 55 and Over, 1982* (Social Security Administration, 1984), tables 44 and 46, pp. 78 and 80.

Reprinted from testimony of Alicia H. Munnell, "Retirement Income Security in the United States," presented before the House Subcommittee on Social Security and Subcommittee on Oversight of the Committee on Ways and Means, 18 July 1985.

In short, for most elderly households today, Social Security provides the foundation for economic security, which is generally supplemented by other sources of income. But what about tomorrow?

The Need for Social Security in the Future

Might other sources of income in old age expand in the foreseeable future so as to greatly reduce or eliminate the need for Social Security? Those who have examined this question almost always conclude that not only is Social Security the cornerstone of income for today's elderly, but there is also a need for it to remain so in the future.

The 1981 National Commission on Social Security reviewed alternatives to Social Security and concluded that none could provide the same certainty of benefits and widespread protection as Social Security.[38] The 1982 National Commission on Social Security Reform then studied whether the growth of private pensions might replace (or reduce) the need for Social Security. While never taking a position on the question, this bipartisan commission unanimously recommended in its final report that Congress not alter the fundamental structure or basic principles of Social Security, while it also rejected proposals to make Social Security voluntary or means-tested.[39] Similarly, the 1979 President's Commission on Pension Policy endorsed Social Security's current role as the cornerstone of the retirement income system in that it provides a minimum floor of protection for the aged; at the same time, the commission also called for the expansion of employee pensions as supplements to Social Security.[40]

As already noted, Social Security is the only part of the old-age income security system that extends protection to nearly every worker and his or her family. Currently, about 95 percent of the work force is covered by the program. Workers do not lose protection as they move from job to job. Because of the near universality of coverage, upon reaching retirement ages nearly all workers and their spouses will have earned the right to benefits. Further, wage and price indexing together protect covered workers and recipients against economic changes over which they have no control, thereby making Social Security highly predictable. These two factors—the nearly universal coverage of Social Security and the predictability of Social Security income—virtually insure that Social Security will continue as the cornerstone of the old-age income security system for the foreseeable future.

The benefit formula provides for wage indexing of earnings and for price indexing of benefits. These indexing procedures currently play and will continue to play a major role in helping families maintain their prior standards of living. The wage-indexing provision essentially works to guarantee a pension that bears a constant relationship to preretirement standards of living. Once received, benefits are generally price indexed to adjust for changes in the cost of living. This price-indexing feature—the COLA—virtually assures that benefits will maintain their value throughout retirement years.

In table 4.6 we present past trends and projections of monthly benefits and replacement rates for three types of hypothetical workers retiring at normal retirement ages from 1940 through 2050. The income figures are all presented in 1985 dollars so as to facilitate comparison between benefit levels in different years. The projections are based on

Alternative IIB—the most commonly accepted set of demographic and economic assumptions—which was used in the 1985 Trustees Report's analysis of Social Security's financing. They include the assumption that beginning in 1994, wage increases will be 1.5 percent greater than price increases.[44] Alternative IIB generally assumes slightly smaller increases in real wages prior to 1994.

The data in table 4.6 illustrate why Social Security will continue as the foundation of the old-age income security system. The projections suggest that real benefit amounts—that is, benefits after adjusting for changes in the cost of living—will be substantially greater in the future, although the percent of income replacement for workers at different earning levels will remain essentially the same (and, as we have noted, rates of return will generally be lower).

Because replacement rates* resulting from the wage-indexing features of the law are stable, the anticipated real growth in wages translates into larger retirement benefits. And Social Security will continue to replace roughly the same proportion of prior earnings in the future as it does now. Consequently, its importance to individuals as a source of retirement income is not likely to diminish.

SOCIAL SECURITY IS A GOOD DEAL

Previous discussion suggests that Social Security is a good deal for all generations. Because some analysts question this proposition and because public confidence in the future of the program has declined significantly during the past 10 years, it is important to both acknowledge and discuss two major criticisms of the program—first, that some people, especially the young, will not get their "money's worth" out of Social Security, and second, that Social Security is financially untenable over the long run.

---

*Replacement rates measure the proportion of preretirement earnings that is replaced by a worker's retirement pension(s).[41] Retirees are usually in lower tax brackets, no longer need to save for retirement,[42] and have somewhat reduced financial responsibilities due to such factors as their children being grown and their mortgages being paid off. Consequently, the maintenance of prior living standards does not require pensions to replace 100 percent of prior earnings. Replacement rates that maintain prior standards of living will vary by such factors as prior earning levels, marital status, and individual circumstances. For middle-income workers, replacing 65 percent to 70 percent of gross preretirement earnings will generally maintain living standards.[43] Lower-income workers will need to replace a somewhat larger proportion of preretirement income mainly because they are generally in low tax brackets during their working years. The reverse is true for higher-income workers.

Table 4.6
Social Security Benefits (in 1985 dollars)
for Workers Retiring at Normal Retirement Age[1]

Year Reaching Normal Retirement Age (NRA)	Normal Retirement Age[2]	For Hypothetical Worker with Low Earnings Throughout Worklife[3,4]		For Hypothetical Worker with Average Earnings Throughout Worklife		For Hypothetical Worker with Maximum Taxable Earnings Throughout Worklife	
		Monthly Benefits	Replacement Rate[4]	Monthly Benefits	Replacement Rate	Monthly Benefits	Replacement Rate
		($)	(%)	($)	(%)	($)	(%)
1940	65	135	39.8	190	26.3	314	16.5
1950	65	103	33.5	145	15.8	200	18.1
1960	65	281	45.0	386	33.3	429	29.8
1970	65	325	42.7	463	34.3	522	29.2
1980	65	384	59.0	583	47.1	740	30.0
1990	65	376	68.3	575	41.6	777	24.2
2000	65	423	66.3	659	41.2	950	25.3
2010	66	461	62.7	753	40.9	1155	26.7
2020	66	509	60.2	868	40.9	1360	27.4
2030	67	563	57.8	993	40.6	1553	27.2
2040	67	648	57.7	1144	40.6	1788	27.1
2050	67	746	57.7	1318	40.6	2059	27.1

[1] Projected benefits and replacement rates for steady workers are based on the intermediate (Alternative IIB) economic assumption used in the *1985 Annual Report of the Board of Trustees of the Federal Old-Age and Survivors Insurance and Disability Insurance Trust Funds*. Earnings are assumed to be at specified levels at ages 21-64 (or 65 or 66, as NRA rises).

[2] Normal Retirement Age refers to the age of first eligibility for unreduced benefits. It is scheduled to increase gradually from 65 to 67 over a 27-year period beginning in 2000.

[3] "Low earnings" is defined as 2080 hours per year at federal minimum wage.

[4] "Replacement rate" is defined as initial monthly benefit times 12, divided by earnings in previous year.

Source: Bruce D. Schobel, Office of the Actuary, Social Security Administration, December 1985.

The Question of Money's Worth*

The issue of whether people receive their money's worth out of Social Security usually comes up in three different ways. Critics have suggested that Social Security is unfair and a poor investment because 1) future cohorts of retirees will receive smaller rates of return on the taxes they and their employers paid on their behalf than those received by persons retiring earlier in the history of the system; 2) within cohorts, some individuals and groups receive higher rates of return than others;

---

*See chapter 8 for additional discussion of the money's worth issue.

and 3) rates of return on alternative private investments are potentially higher. For instance, in recent congressional testimony, Harvard economist Martin Feldstein, formerly President Reagan's chair of the Council of Economic Advisors, stated:

> The principal reason why Social Security was such a good deal for the early cohorts of retirees is that the Social Security payroll tax rate rose from only 2 percent at the start of the program to more than 10 percent today. Since Social Security is financed on a pay-as-you-go basis, the rise in the payroll tax rate and therefore in total Social Security tax collections made it possible to increase benefits at a very rapid rate.
>
> In the future, Social Security will no longer be a good deal for the vast majority of workers. Young people who have begun work in the past decade or who will enter the work force in the future will not get nearly as much back for their Social Security contributions as they could get by investing those funds in government bonds or corporate securities.[45]

Broadly speaking, the observations of Feldstein and other critics about the declining rates of return in Social Security are correct. However, the conclusion that Social Security is a poor investment is very questionable. Further, the other widely drawn conclusion—that it is unfair to younger persons—depends on the lenses one uses to define fairness and is at best the result of focusing exclusively on individual equity to the neglect of other goals.

First, it is important to understand why rates of return are declining and what the alternative was. In the early years of Social Security, decisions were made to enable workers nearing retirement age to receive benefits even though they had made relatively small contributions. This also applied to subsequent benefit liberalizations in that workers nearing retirement age became eligible for these new benefits, too. This resulted in relatively high rates of return for workers retiring early in the life of the program and even for current retirees. As discussed, this practice of allowing workers nearing retirement to reap the benefit of a new retirement plan (or of improvements in an existing plan) is similar to that which by and large prevails in private industry when a private pension plan is established or liberalized. Because the basic structure and major benefit liberalizations in Social Security have generally been in place for a number of years, future retirees will not reap such high rates of return. However, the alternative—failure to blanket in workers nearing retirement age—would have compromised the system's goal of adequacy. Further, it would have raised other issues related to fairness since the anticipated economic welfare of cohorts nearing retirement age has usually been less than that for cohorts whose retirements are many years in the future. Additionally, its effectiveness in response to a serious social problem—the reality that, in the first half of the century, the majority of the elderly were poor with most living in destitution—would have been very limited. A Social Security system without benefits for those near retirement would quite simply have perpetuated the problem.

Second, while acknowledging that rates of return have declined substantially, it is important to recognize that, under nearly every set of reasonable assumptions, future cohorts of retirees can expect to receive positive rates of return.[46]

Third, and most important, it must also be recognized that Social Security is a complex system involving *many* policy goals, only one of which—individual equity—requires benefits received to be comparable to the amount of payroll tax contributed. Because individual equity is one of the goals, it is reasonable to evaluate the program, at least in part, from this vantage point. The problem arises, however, when broad conclusions about the program's fairness or value are reached based on such a limited measure as its rate of return, without also recognizing the importance of other equally (many would say more) important policy goals such as adequacy, dignity, insurance against risk, and program stability.

For example, those who suggest that Social Security is unfair because the rates of return for high-income persons are generally lower than those for moderate-income persons with families overlook the fact that social insurance is designed to provide minimally adequate benefits for moderate- and low-income persons and their families. The relatively lower rates of return for higher-income persons is the price paid for incorporating the goal of adequacy, which is so fundamental to the program.

Finally, in discussing the fairness of Social Security, one must always keep in mind the value of the many types of benefits that flow from the program. Brookings economist Henry Aaron points out:

> the range of benefits that social security offers cannot be
> replicated now in the private sector because no package of

private benefits is fully indexed against inflation. It has been shown that a judicious selection of private securities could have yielded a portfolio that would have behaved as if it were indexed. But there is no guarantee that this portfolio will continue to behave as if it were indexed. Furthermore, the real rate of return on such a portfolio was close to zero. . . . [It] is possible to argue that the market has indicated that it would accept indexed bonds with a zero rate of return and that a zero discount rate should be used in evaluating social security benefits; by such a criterion, all cohorts now and for the foreseeable future would receive social security benefits worth far more than the taxes they pay.[47]

The Stability of Financing

Despite generally widespread support for the program among all age groups, considerable skepticism exists within the public at large, especially among the young, about the future of Social Security. A recent poll conducted for the AARP indicates that 52 percent of the public aged 25 and over (67 percent of those 25 through 34) are not confident about the program's future viability.[48] Munnell points out that such skepticism

> may be a natural reaction to scare stories about social security going broke that appeared before the passage of the 1983 amendments [to the Social Security Act], but it is not supported by the facts. According to the most recent report of the system's Board of Trustees, the social security program is adequately financed for both the near-term and for decades ahead. . . .
>
> [Further,] even under unrealistically pessimistic demographic and economic assumptions, social security revenues will be more than adequate to cover promised benefits until 2020 and, under the central assumptions, the system is adequately financed until 2050. In short, social security will be here for today's workers when it comes time for them to retire.[49]

Since the passage of the 1983 amendments that responded to the financing problems of Social Security, experts[50] and politicians of both parties have generally agreed the program is adequately financed. And while none would suggest that there will never be problems in the future and many would advocate changes in particular aspects of the program, there appears to be a fairly widespread consensus within the nation's business community as well that Social Security is now adequately financed. For example, 111 key private sector pension professionals recently signed a statement in the *New York Times* (11 August 1985) expressing their complete confidence in Social Security:

> In recognition of the Fiftieth Anniversary of Social Security, we the undersigned wish to pay tribute to its indispensable role in providing economic security.
>
> Social Security provides the bedrock of America's income security programs. That is our message to America as private sector pension professionals.
>
> The Social Security system operates soundly. The trust funds and scheduled future taxes have been designed to assure that Social Security will be able to pay its promised benefits in the future, just as it has always done in the past. They and the broad support of the electorate insure that Social Security is secure now—and for the future. Social Security works. We have complete confidence in Social Security.[51]

In short, although serious financing problems emerged during the late 1970s and early 1980s, the passage of remedial legislation in 1983 resolved them, assuring that Social Security will meet its commitments for the foreseeable future.*

CONCLUSION

All generations have a common stake in Social Security, an intergenerational transfer based on public policy. Social Security provides a rational, dignified, and stable means of protecting against certain risks to economic well-being to which individuals and family members are

---

*It is also sometimes suggested that Social Security will be unable to meet its long-term commitments because of projected changes in the "aged dependency ratio," a measure of the number of persons aged 18 through 64 for every 100 persons aged 65 and over. See chapter 8 for a discussion of why analysis based on the aged dependency ratio sometimes leads to the misleading conclusion that the nation will be unable to sustain programs that respond to the needs of a growing elderly population.

exposed over the course of their lives—mainly the loss of income due to retirement, disability, or death of a breadwinner. When the program is examined from a long-term perspective, the benefits and costs of Social Security are shown to be distributed widely across all generations. Not only will Social Security remain the heart of the nation's retirement income program for the foreseeable future, but—all things considered—it remains a good deal for all covered workers and their families.

Although our focus here is on Social Security, many of the same points could have been made about other intergenerational transfers based on public policies (such as education). The broader point to be reiterated is that, in a highly interdependent society such as ours, these intergenerational transfers are critical responses to needs that exist across the life course. Because of our interdependence, the benefits that flow from these policies do not accrue only to the groups to which they are targeted at one point in time (e.g., children in the case of public education; the elderly, disabled, and survivors [and their families] in the case of Social Security) but to *all* groups over time.

We do not conclude from these observations that such transfers are flawless and should never be changed. On the contrary, because of the critical functions they serve in society and because demographic and economic change is an ongoing process, it is essential that these policies be carefully reviewed and policy options vigorously debated. Our concern is that those who are considering changes need to understand who benefits from these policies and the common stake that exists in these intergenerational transfers.

Notes

1. Yankelovich, Skelly, and White, Inc., *A Fifty-Year Report Card on the Social Security System: The Attitudes of the American Public* (Washington, D.C.: AARP, 1985).

2. American Council of Life Insurance, Health Insurance Association of America, National Council of Senior Citizens, National Council on the Aging, *The Prime Life Generation* (Washington, D.C.: American Council of Life Insurance and Health Insurance Association of America, 1985), unpublished data.

3. Lawrence H. Thompson, "The Social Security Reform Debate," *Journal of Economic Literature* 21 (December 1983): 1463.

4. James H. Schulz, "To Old Folks with Love: Aged Income Maintenance in America," *The Gerontologist* 25 (October 1985): 470.

5. Wilbur J. Cohen, article in *Social Security: Universal or Selective*, ed. W. J. Cohen and M. Friedman (Washington, D.C.: American Enterprise Institute for Public Policy Research, 1972).

6. Robert M. Ball, *Social Security Today and Tomorrow* (New York: Columbia University Press, 1978), 9.

7. Reinhard A. Hohaus, "Equity, Adequacy, and Related Factors in Old Age Security," in *Social Security Programs, Problems, and Policies*, ed. William Haber and Wilbur J. Cohen (Homewood, Ill.: Richard D. Irwin, Inc., 1960), 62.

8. Robert J. Myers, *Social Security*, 3d ed. (Homewood, Ill.: Richard D. Irwin, Inc., 1985), 11.

9. Ball, *Social Security Today and Tomorrow*, 7.

10. Myers, *Social Security*, 14.

11. Thompson, "The Social Security Reform Debate," 1460.

12. Brown, *Essays on Social Security*, 31-32.

13. Schulz, *Economics of Aging*, 71.

14. Myers, *Social Security*, 12.

15. Ball, *Social Security Today and Tomorrow*, 5-6; Brown, *Essays on Social Security*, 31-32; Myers, *Social Security*, 16-17.

16. Ball, *Social Security Today and Tomorrow*, 5; Myers, *Social Security*, 16-17.

17. Press Office, Social Security Administration, Woodlawn, Md.

18. Ibid.

19. Ibid.

20. Ibid.

21. See, for example, Board of Trustees, *1985 Annual Report*.

22. Robert M. Ball, visiting scholar, Center for the Study of Social Policy, Washington, D.C., personal communication, March 1985.

23. Board of Trustees, *1985 Annual Report*, 30.

24. Unpublished data, Social Security Administration, Office of Research, Statistics and International Policy; Grad, *Income of the Population 55 and Over, 1982*, 66.

25. William C. Birdsall, "Private Transfers and Shared Living: An Exploratory Analysis of Clan Support" (Ann Arbor, Mich.: Institute for Social Research, University of Michigan, 1982, Mimeographed).

26. U.S. Department of Housing and Urban Development, *1977 Statistical Yearbook* (Washington, D.C.: U.S. GPO, 1978), 247.

27. Bureau of the Census, "Characteristics of Households and Persons Receiving Selected and Non-Cash Benefits: 1982," *Current Population Reports*, ser. P-60, no. 143 (Washington, D.C.: U.S. GPO, 1983), 87.

28. Estimates based on calculations provided by Bruce D. Schobel, Office of the Actuary, Social Security Administration, December 1985.

29. Eric R. Kingson, *Social Security and You* (New York: Ballantine Books, 1983), 15.

30. Robert L. Clark et al., *Inflation and the Economic Well-Being of the Elderly* (Baltimore, Md.: The Johns Hopkins University Press, 1984), 10.

31. Alicia H. Munnell, "Retirement Income Security in the United States," testimony presented before the House Subcommittee on Social Security and Subcommittee on Oversight of the Committee on Ways and Means, 18 July 1985.

32. Bureau of Labor Statistics, *Handbook of Labor Statistics* (Washington, D.C.: U.S. GPO, 1983), 16; Bureau of Labor Statistics, *Employment and Earnings* (Washington, D.C.: U.S. GPO, 1985), table 3.

33. Alicia H. Munnell, *The Economics of Private Pensions* (Washington, D.C.: The Brookings Institution, 1982), 11.

34. Schulz, *Economics of Aging*, 149.

35. Munnell, "Retirement Income Security."

36. Linda Drazga Maxfield and Virginia P. Reno, "Distribution of Income Sources of Recent Retirees: Findings from the New Beneficiary Survey," *Social Security Bulletin* 48, no. 1 (January 1985): 13.

37. Ibid., 12.

38. National Commission on Social Security, *Final Report of the National Commission on Social Security: Social Security in America's Future* (Washington, D.C.: U.S. GPO, 1981), 35-51.

39. National Commission on Social Security Reform, *Report of the National Commission on Social Security Reform* (Washington, D.C.: U.S. GPO, 1983).

40. President's Commission on Pension Policy, *Coming of Age: Toward a National Retirement Income Policy* (Washington, D.C.: U.S. GPO, 1981), 41-52.

41. Schulz, *Economics of Aging*, 95.

42. Ibid., 74.

43. Ibid.

44. Board of Trustees, *1985 Annual Report*, 28.

45. Martin Feldstein, "Fundamental Reform of Social Security," testimony presented before the House Subcommittee on Social Security and Subcommittee on Oversight of the Committee on Ways and Means, 18 July 1985.

46. For additional information on the value of Social Security to future cohorts of retirees, see Henry J. Aaron, *Economic Effects of Social Security* (Washington, D.C.: The Brookings Institution, 1982); Myers, *Social Security*; Robert J. Myers, "Do Young People Get Their Money's-Worth from Social Security?" (Study Group on Social Security, New York, 1985, Mimeographed).

47. Aaron, *Economic Effects of Social Security*, 75-76.

48. Yankelovich, Skelly, and White, Inc., *A Fifty-Year Report Card*.

49. Munnell, "Retirement Income Security."

50. See, for example, Robert J. Myers, "Will Social Security Have Another Financing Crisis Soon?" *Benefits Quarterly* 1, no. 1 (n.d.): 22-25; Robert M. Ball, "Fifty Years of Social Security," testimony presented before the Senate Special Committee on Aging, Pittsburgh, Pa., 13 August 1985; James Tobin, "The Future of Social Security: One Economist's Assessment," *Social Security: Project on*

the Federal Social Role, Working Paper 4 (Washington, D.C.: National Conference on Social Welfare, 1985); Munnell, "Retirement Income Security."

51. Study Group on Social Security, "Social Security: A Declaration of Confidence and Support by Private Pension Professionals," advertisement, *New York Times*, 11 August 1985.

5

The Common Stake In Research on Aging

SOCIETAL intergenerational transfers are for the most part due to both private- and public-sector decisions, such as 1) whether or not to promote research in particular areas (e.g., aging, computer technology, fusion technology), 2) what type of research to encourage within particular areas, and 3) how much resources to direct at particular topics. Thus, they can be seen to shape the quality of life for current and subsequent generations as well as the nature of the problems and opportunities these generations (will) confront. Economic growth, for example, usually results from private decisions (e.g., to risk capital) and public decisions (e.g., to give tax incentives), which in turn influence the decision to invest in plants and machinery, in training the work force, and in developing new technologies and products. Because investment requires withholding some present consumption in exchange for future growth, decisions made to (or not to) invest result in transfers of resources between generations, transfers which thus help shape the future and our response to it. Investments in research on aging constitute a particularly persuasive example of the commonality of benefits flowing from societal intergenerational transfers.

THE CHALLENGE, THE OPPORTUNITIES, AND THE NEED FOR RESEARCH

The elderly—especially the very old—have been growing and will continue to grow both in numbers and as a percent of the total population (see chap. 2). Further, not only are the overwhelming majority of Americans now expected to reach age 65, but life expectancy at age

65—currently about 14.7 years for men and 19.1 years for women—is projected to increase.[1]

While these trends indicate the success of our society, they also present a new and multidimensional challenge. This challenge includes 1) preventing, postponing, limiting, and managing the functional disabilities associated with the chronic illnesses that often accompany old age, especially advanced old age; 2) finding ways to meet the income and health care needs of the elderly through both individual effort and private- and public-sector programs; 3) slowing down the expected rate of increase in costs—especially health care costs—associated with an aging society; and 4) developing ways to increase the likelihood that the years being added to life expectancy are both satisfying and productive. Finally, this challenge also involves—and indeed cannot avoid—doing all this while improving the quality of life for *all* members of society, regardless of age.

Investing in research on aging is one of the principal ways of responding to this challenge. Because an aging society is a new phenomenon, there is little experience to guide future actions. Public and private decision makers need information about 1) demographic, economic, health, and other trends among the elderly; 2) the kinds and levels of needs for services these trends will create; and 3) the kinds and numbers of personnel required to meet these needs.[2] Of greater importance is the need for new knowledge, which may alter some of the less attractive aspects of an aging society (e.g., the projected increase in demand for and level of expenditures directed at caring for the functionally disabled elderly) and help maximize the opportunities emerging from it. Before we explore the potential returns on such an investment, it is useful to review some of the strides research on aging has already made.

Research in Response to the Challenge of an Aging Society

One clear implication of population trends associated with an aging society is that there will be a greater need for long-term care services for functionally disabled elderly persons residing both in institutions and at home (see chap. 3 for a discussion of future trends and estimates). To avoid presenting an unrealistically optimistic view of the potential of research to reduce the costs and personal suffering associated with certain debilitating illnesses, two words of caution are needed. First, for those elderly requiring long-term care, decline in functional capacity is usually a result of many social factors (e.g., loss of spouse) and many medical factors as well. Of the latter, for example, a typical nursing home patient is likely to have several debilitating chronic ailments (e.g., Alzheimer's disease, arthritis, incontinence, and heart disease). Consequently, for the individual and society, the benefits of medical progress in treating, delaying the onset of, or even eliminating a particular disease are likely to be somewhat offset by the presence and perhaps eventual increase in severity of other diseases. Second, even with significant research breakthroughs, the growing numbers of elderly and very old imply that the costs of long-term care for individuals, families, and society will increase.

Even so, new knowledge may lead to ways of reducing the debilitating impacts of chronic illness for some elderly and their families as well as some associated costs to individuals, families, and society. Research on the problem of incontinence, which afflicts an estimated 2.6 to 4.7 million elderly persons,[3] could significantly reduce the number of people in nursing homes and allow some incontinent individuals (who might otherwise have been institutionalized) to remain at home in the care of relatives for a greater length of time.[4] In fact, if research and education efforts have only a 5 percent impact on nursing home admissions during the next 20 years, conservative estimates suggest nursing home expenditures would be reduced by about $1.125 million per day.[5] Similarly, investments in pharmaceutical and basic research are likely to "provide new therapies for many of the conditions that impair the functional ability of many of today's elderly... [and] lead to significant reductions in the severity of chronic illness among the elderly and in the cost of health care for this growing segment of the U.S. population."[6]

One area where some progress is being made—and more is needed—concerns Alzheimer's disease and related dementias. Although "the great majority of people maintain good mental functioning into their later years, the proportions of those who acquire a significant degree of dementia rise rapidly among the very old," with an estimated one in five persons aged 80 and over having a serious, irreversible dementia.[7] Moreover, an estimated 30 percent to 50 percent of patients in nursing homes have Alzheimer's disease.[8]

To date, gerontological research on Alzheimer's disease has provided new evidence that the nucleus basalis, the part of the brain that directs brain cells to communicate with one another, is the first area to degenerate.[9] In addition, such research has 1) shown that carefully structured environments and daily schedules can assist patients and their families in managing this disease; 2) led to increasing recognition on the clinical level of the absolute necessity of ruling out "potentially treatable causes of dementia before concluding that a person has Alzheimer's disease''; 3) begun testing the effectiveness of pharmaceutical approaches to treating Alzheimer's;[10] and 4) begun to identify its organic basis.

Between now and the year 2000, an approximately 50 percent increase is projected in the number of nursing home beds needed. Half or more of this increase[11] and much more of the increased need for community-based long-term care services are related to the expected needs of persons experiencing severe dementia. Plainly, as a society, we have a stake in investments made now in basic and applied research that will produce information which—through prevention, reduction of incidence, and/or treatment—may lessen the impact on individuals, families, and society of this and other devastating diseases.

Research in Response to the Opportunities Presented by an Aging Society

The challenge of an aging society also involves developing ways to increase the likelihood that the years being added to life expectancy are satisfying and productive for both individuals and society. Investing in research may 1) help ensure the best possible health for future cohorts of the elderly; 2) identify ways to ensure that the elderly and very old can continue to contribute to the development of society through work and community involvement; and 3) identify the opportunities society has for using the talents of a growing and increasingly better educated older population.

For example, research has shown that disease prevention, health promotion, and proper nutrition can greatly increase the likelihood of reaching old age in good health and of maintaining one's health in old age. (Of course, this kind of research has helped improve the health of everyone along the way.) Exercising and not smoking can have beneficial effects at any age. Similarly, proper nutrition can reduce the risk of diabetes, coronary heart disease, and stroke.[12] Additional research can provide new ways of promoting health in old age, thereby improving the quality of life and possibly reducing anticipated health care costs to society. Clearly, the payoffs that emerge from such research are widely distributed across generations.

Using the talents of the elderly serves the interests of society as well as of the elderly. With more people projected to live longer, it seems likely that a significant portion of the future elderly may be both willing and able to work longer. Research being conducted today can provide the information needed—including developing ways to maintain older workers beyond the normal retirement age—to assist employers and employees in adjusting to an aging work force. In short, the research on aging done in response to the challenge of an aging society is an intergenerational transfer that will potentially play a large role in shaping the future.

ALL GENERATIONS BENEFIT FROM RESEARCH ON AGING

The common stake in research on aging also arises from the benefits that accrue to all generations from such research. Clearly, current cohorts of the elderly often benefit directly from such research, but indirect benefits also accrue to persons of all ages. For example, indirect benefits may include decreased health care costs to taxpayers and reduced caregiving costs—financial, emotional, and physical—to families who provide support to older relatives.

Further, the actual benefits of most research on aging for the most part accrue primarily to those who are not at all old. For instance, research on osteoporosis, a condition particularly noticeable among postmenopausal women, has resulted in a prescription for preventive maintenance involving diet (e.g., maintaining proper calcium intake), exercise to develop and maintain bone mass, and other life-style factors for women of all ages.[13]

Indeed, research focused on a particular concern of an aging society may benefit only *future* cohorts of the elderly. But although today's elderly and perhaps even today's middle-aged *may never benefit personally* from some of this research, the knowledge that flows from their investments in research will be transferred as a legacy to future generations in society. In a very fundamental way, then, research on aging is an intergenerational transfer of great benefit to persons of all ages as well as to those yet to be born. It is an investment in our common future.

We have focused on research on aging as one example of societal intergenerational transfers for three reasons: 1) it ties closely to the theme of this report; 2) it is an area of particular interest to the authors; and 3) it is, in our opinion, one of the principal means of responding to the challenge of an aging society.

However, had we chosen other societal intergenerational transfers (e.g., economic growth, environmental conservation, governmental deficits, support for the arts, promotion of research in other areas), some general conclusions would remain the same:

- Societal intergenerational transfers are fundamental to the progress and continuity of each generation in society.

- Younger persons and subsequent generations will potentially benefit more than older persons from transfers initiated today as well as those initiated in the past.

- To respond to a variety of challenges in the future, it is necessary to make a variety of investments today.

Undeniably, all generations have a common stake in intergenerational transfers. To understand this leads naturally to a broader view of the implications of policies directed at any one age group (e.g., children, the middle-aged, the elderly).

Notes

1. Board of Trustees, *1985 Annual Report*, 30.

2. John M. Cornman, executive director, The Gerontological Society of America, "Statement of Jack Cornman," testimony presented before the Senate Committee on Appropriations, Subcommittee on Labor, Health and Human Services, and Education, 27 April 1984.

3. OTA, *Technology and Aging in America*, 9.

4. Ibid.

5. Tom Hickey, "Statement of Tom Hickey, Dr. P.H.," testimony presented before the Senate Committee on Appropriations, Subcommittee on Labor, Health and Human Services, and Education, 14 May 1985.

6. OTA, *Technology and Aging in America*, 457.

7. T. Franklin Williams, "Statement by T. Franklin Williams, M.D.," testimony presented before the House Committee on Energy and Commerce, Subcommittee on Health and the Environment, and the House Select Committee on Aging, Subcommittee on Health and Long-Term Care, 3 August 1983.

8. OTA, *Technology and Aging in America*, 67.

9. National Institutes of Health (hereafter referred to as NIH), "Special Report on Aging 1984," prepared for congressional hearings for fiscal year 1985 appropriations for NIH (Washington, D.C.: U.S. Department of Health and Human Services, 1985), 17.

10. T. Franklin Williams, "Statement."

11. Ibid.

12. OTA, *Technology and Aging in America*, 10-12.

13. Ibid., 97-100; for additional information concerning current research on osteoporosis, see NIH, "Special Report on Aging 1984."

6

The Life Course Perspective: Implications For Public Policy

Our LIVES are characterized by both continuity with our pasts and ongoing change. The sum total of who we are depends variously on how personal circumstances (e.g., abilities, when we were born, and who our parents are) interact with, and are shaped by, social structure (e.g., mechanisms such as the market economy by which society distributes rewards), historical events (e.g., war, depressions), and social policy.[1] Although many factors that influence human development are largely outside our immediate control (e.g., new technologies), we neither are nor become simply passive responses to society. Within the constraints imposed by society, we actively shape our lives through personal decisions and through decisions that in turn shape society.

The above ideas are central to the life course perspective, which also incorporates the idea that each "new birth cohort potentially ages through a different trajectory of life events, brought about by the impress of sociohistorical change and by individual reactions to it."[2]

This chapter builds on one part of the life course perspective—that which focuses on continuity over the life course—to emphasize how outcomes in old age are related to experiences earlier in life. Before going further, however, it is important to reiterate that the life course theory also emphasizes change; expanding on this notion, social and physical scientists generally agree that nearly all individuals retain the capacity to change throughout their lives—even in advanced old age—and that interventions directed at every age can produce change.

OLD AGE IS PARTIALLY SHAPED
BY WHAT HAPPENS EARLIER

If quality of life in old age is at least partially shaped by experiences earlier in life, those interested in planning for future cohorts of the elderly need to consider how interventions and experiences throughout life affect people when they become elderly. As the research agenda in this report indicates, increasing our knowledge in this area is one of the major challenges to research on aging (see the afterword). While there is much we do not know, this section draws on existing research to show how quality of life in old age—especially economic and health status—is partially determined by the effects of social structure, social policies, biomedical events, and personal decisions made prior to old age.

The Economic Status of the Elderly and the Life Course

The link between lifelong experiences and the economic welfare of current and future elderly cohorts is quite easy to demonstrate. Social structure and social policies interact across people's lives to influence their economic welfare in old age. For instance, the economy is probably the most important factor in determining the economic well-being of the elderly.[3] The fact that current cohorts of the elderly are, as a whole, better off than those who preceded them is largely the result of economic growth that has typified the post-World War II period. Not only do the retirement incomes of these workers reflect the generally higher earnings they realized throughout their lives, but economic growth has also permitted expansions of Social Security and of private and public-employee pension protections. The lesson for those interested in the economic welfare of future cohorts of the elderly is that each cohort's economic welfare in old age is related to the economic growth that occurs throughout their lives.

Social policies also interact with the economy to affect economic outcomes in old age. The favorable tax decisions, court cases, and wage-price controls during the Korean War period[4] contributed to the expansion of the private pension system that is so critical to the economic welfare of a modest but significant subpopulation of today's retirees.

For individuals, both the presence and magnitude of Social Security, private and public-employee pensions, and asset income are related to their employment histories. Benefits under Social Security reflect prior earnings on which payroll taxes were paid. Consequently, workers with steady employment in better-paying jobs generally receive larger benefits (although this is somewhat modified by the provisions in the law that

108

allow proportionately larger benefits for lower-income workers). Similarly, it is not surprising that the current elderly who are members of minority groups and/or who are female tend to receive lower retirement incomes. The lifelong effects of discrimination—overt and institutionalized—generally limited the economic opportunities of these groups while they were young and middle-aged. This, in turn, resulted in less economic security in old age than would otherwise have been the case.

Private and public-employee benefits are even more directly related to prior work histories than is Social Security. First, private and public-employee pension coverage is associated with higher-paying occupations, often those in highly capitalized and unionized industries, and in civil service, professional, and managerial occupations. Second, the availability and size of employee pensions are related—even more than under Social Security—to long-term steady employment and prior earnings of retirees. Third, in addition to employee benefits, income from assets, which is partially a result of lifelong investments, is also often linked to earnings.

Researchers have begun to show how outcomes in old age may relate to lifelong processes. Building on work that seeks to explain the relationship between occupational attainment for young and middle-aged workers and factors such as family background and education, two analysts conclude that the factors that explain retirement income—education, occupation, and marital status—"are the same ones that determine income before retirement."[5] In fact, the research of Joel Leon, a professor at Washington University, indicates that as "early as age 35, the school dropout, the person with limited job success, and the dependable worker in small 'mom and pop' businesses already face difficult retirements."[6] These and other findings lead him to conclude that

> [the] process that leads to economic status in retirement begins at birth. Race, gender, and the socio-economic position of one's parents, factors clearly beyond anyone's control, explain many of the differences. While not the complete explanation, they describe how people are launched into trajectories that ultimately determine dignity or despair in old age.[7]

In short, the lesson to be learned from research is that, while events occurring early and throughout life are not the only factors that explain levels of retirement income, economic well-being in old age is, at least in part, related to early life experiences. Further, the discussion suggests that specific policies that shape educational and employment opportunities have implications for the economic well-being of people when they retire and are therefore important to those concerned with the economic status of new cohorts of the elderly.

The Health Status of the Elderly and the Life Course

Social structure, social policy, biomedical events, and personal decisions at all points across people's lives can and do influence health status in old age in terms of who reaches old age, longevity in old age, and health-related quality of life. The reasons for increasing longevity and the causes of illness in old age are many and complex. Consequently, we do not mean to suggest here that most illnesses in old age primarily result from lifelong processes or that we know how closely related many illnesses are to life course events. As in our discussion of the economic status of the elderly, we mostly intend to show simply that a link exists between lifelong experiences and outcomes in old age—in this case, the longevity and health of the elderly.

The fact that today more people reach old age can be attributed primarily to both long-term declines in infant mortality and improvements in the environment and medical care.[8] Declines in infant mortality—most notably in the first third of the twentieth century—are largely a result of improved prenatal care and nutrition, better delivery techniques, sanitation, better living standards, and better postnatal care and nutrition.[9] The probability that children and young adults will reach old age has also been increased by improvements in medical care—especially by the development of antibiotic treatment for infections[10]—and by public health measures such as sanitation and immunizations. Plainly, without such social progress, many among today's and tomorrow's elderly would have had their lives cut short.

Since 1960, life expectancy at 65 and over has increased substantially. The causes of declining mortality rates among the elderly, while not fully understood, seem related to declines in "incidences of and mortality from heart diseases and stroke" and quite probably to treatment of hypertension, increased access to medical care, and changes in life-style and diet.[11] In fact, basic research supports the idea that diet can affect longevity; for example, researchers found that manipulation of diet early in the lives of laboratory rats increases life expectancy and maximum life span.[12]

The effects of social structure, social policies, and personal decisions on both aggregate and individual life expectancies are easily demonstrated. In the case of social structure, for example, age- and sex-adjusted mortality rates are higher for blacks than for whites in all categories under age 65; this means that, at any given age prior to 65, black men and women are more likely to die than their white counterparts. This is generally considered to be the result of the lower standard of living, harder working conditions, greater exposure to health risks, and more limited access to health care.[13]

In terms of social policies, certainly people of all ages, including today's and tomorrow's elderly, have benefited from those that ensure good sanitary practices as well as from medical research that has resulted in life-saving procedures, medications, and immunizations. For example, findings that asbestosis and mesothelioma (a disease of the lining of the body cavity)—which generally affect people when they are middle-aged or older—usually result from exposure to asbestos in the workplace have led to efforts to eliminate asbestos in the workplace, including children's schools.[14] Similarly, publicly supported research has clearly identified the increased risk of mortality at all ages (even to the fetus) from smoking, thereby providing individuals with the knowledge needed to increase their own probabilities of survival at every age.

Finally, in terms of personal decisions, smoking provides an excellent example of how outcomes in old age—in this case, lessened probability of reaching old age, of longevity, and/or of general good health—are related to choices often made early in life. Victor Fuchs points out that "the difference in life expectancy at age 24 between non-smokers and those who smoke a pack a day is over six years."[15] Other indications of the harmful impact of smoking can be found in the fact that in 1985, lung cancer was projected to pass breast cancer as the leading cause of cancer death among women—an unfortunate statistic related to increased smoking among women.[16] Since about 90 percent of all smokers begin by age 24—about 50 percent by age 17[17]—mortality outcomes in middle and old age are clearly related to choices made early in life.

Social structure, social policies, and personal decisions at earlier points in the life course may also influence other health outcomes in old age, such as morbidity and functional ability. For example, a case can be made that higher income, access to prenatal care and nutrition, not smoking during pregnancy, higher education of parents, and access to postnatal care all contribute to the probability that children's birth weights will be high enough to reduce the risk of infant mortality or lifelong chronic conditions.

Similarly, the lifelong effects of environment, public health interventions, and personal health behavior can affect the health-related quality of life in old age (and at other ages, too). For example, it is known that

• air pollution, exposure the dust in the workplace, and smoking contribute to lung diseases;[18]

• maintenance of teeth in old age is more likely among those who have had regular dental care throughout their lives, and their continued dental health is associated with proper nutrition in old age;[19]

• adults of all ages may reap psychological benefits from regular exercise;[20] and

• the risk of osteoporosis and related problems (e.g., hip fractures) can be reduced by "supplemental doses of calcium for women prior to menopause" and by exercise to strengthen bones.[21]

The idea that environment affects people's health later in life also finds support in the work of basic researchers; for example, one biologist found that protecting laboratory mice throughout life from normal laboratory odors and noise delayed and even prevented the occurrence of tumors.[22]

Finally, although obvious, it is worth pointing out that health conditions and preventive interventions early in life can affect the health of youth and the middle-aged. While acute (nonchronic) illness in childhood does not necessarily correlate with problems later in life, this is sometimes the case. For example, there is evidence that "perhaps a majority of adults with hearing loss or chronic ear problems had ear problems as children," and that most damage from ear infections occurs before school age.[23] There is also evidence that

• overweight infants become overweight adults;[24]

• the precursors of heart disease in adults—high cholesterol, smoking, hypertension, and inactivity—can be found in childhood;[25] and

• the existence of health problems in childhood is more likely to be related to problems in adulthood among persons who are poor[26] because the poor are more likely to be born at risk (e.g., with low birth weight), to experience greater risk throughout life, and to have less access to ameliorative interventions.[27]

112

SUMMARY AND CONCLUSIONS: IMPLICATIONS FOR PUBLIC POLICY

The quality of life in old age for today's elderly has been shaped by their lifelong experiences. Although in this discussion of continuity we focus on retirement income and physical health outcomes in old age, other examples would lead to many of the same observations. For example, cognitive decline in old age seems greater among those who begin at a lower level of cognitive functioning,[28] so that a case might be made for early and continued learning as a necessary ingredient for lifetime cognitive competence. Further, the quality of life in old age awaiting today's children, youth, and middle-aged adults is and will be shaped by the lifelong effects of social structure, social policies, biomedical events, and personal decisions made prior to their old age.

Several conclusions can thus be drawn:

• *Each age group has a clear stake in social policies that will shape their well-being at all points in the course of life—in part because as they age they will be directly affected by these programs.* For instance, children have a clear stake in policies that affect young, middle-aged, and elderly persons since they will pass through all these stages of the life course themselves.

• *All age groups, at any given time, have a stake in policies that shape the society since each age group is clearly affected by the general well-being of society.*

• *Advocates for the elderly have a stake in social policies affecting* all *age groups—infants, toddlers, children, teenagers, young adults, the middle-aged, and the elderly.* Those concerned with the well-being of both current *and* future cohorts of the elderly need also be concerned with their well-being at all points along the life course. This conclusion is, in fact, inescapable for anyone concerned about the challenge of an aging society.

113

Notes

1. Brim and Kagan, "Constancy and Change," 1-25.

2. Featherman, "Life-Span Perspective," 622.

3. Eric R. Kingson and Richard M. Scheffler, "Aging Issues and Economic Trends for the 1980's," *Inquiry* 18 (Fall 1981): 197.

4. Schulz, *Economics of Aging*, 149-150.

5. John C. Henretta and Richard T. Campbell, "Status Attainment and Status Maintenance: A Study of Stratification in Old Age," *American Sociological Review* 41, no. 6 (1976): 990.

6. Joel Leon, "Reneging on Social Security," *Cleveland* (Ohio) *Plain Dealer*, 11 June 1985; see also Joel Leon, *Final Project Report: Life-Span Models of Economic Status in Retirement*, submitted to the AARP-Andrus Foundation (St. Louis, Mo.: George Warren Brown School of Social Work, Washington University, 1985).

7. Ibid.

8. Richard W. Besdine, "Rational and Successful Health Care of Tomorrow's Elderly: An Academic Perspective," in *Aging 2000: Our Health Care Destiny*, vol. 1, *Biomedical Issues*, ed. Charles M. Gaitz and T. Samorajski (New York: Springer-Verlag, 1985), 260.

9. Ibid.

10. Ibid., 261.

11. Ibid., 261-262.

12. Edward J. Masoro, chairman, Department of Physiology, University of Texas, personal communication, 8 August 1985.

13. Bureau of the Census, "Demographic and Socioeconomic Aspects of Aging," 50.

14. Jordan Tobin, M.D., chief, Gerontology Research Center, National Institute on Aging, personal communication, 12 December 1985.

15. Victor R. Fuchs, *How We Live: An Economic Perspective on Americans from Birth to Death* (Cambridge, Mass.: Harvard University Press, 1983), 111.

16. American Cancer Society, *1985 Cancer Facts and Figures* (New York, 1985).

17. Fuchs, 112.

18. Anthony Robbins, "Creating a Progressive Health Agenda: 1983 Presidential Address," *American Journal of Public Health* 74, no. 8 (n.d.): 777.

19. Bruce J. Baum, "Characteristics of Participants in the Oral Physiology Component of the Baltimore Longitudinal Study of Aging," *Community Dent. Oral Epidemial.* 9 (1981): 128-134.

20. Eric Pfeiffer, "The Mental Health Professional in a Preventive Role," in *Biomedical Issues*, 437.

21. OTA, *Technology and Aging in America*, 9; NIH, "Special Report on Aging 1984," 16.

22. V. Riley, "Psychoneuroendocrine Influences on Immunocompetence and Neoplasia," *Science* 212 (1981): 1100-1109.

23. Barbara Starfield and I.B. Pless, "Physical Health," in *Constancy and Change in Human Development*, ed. Brim and Kagan, 280.

24. Ibid., 282.

25. Ibid., 284.

26. Ibid., 318.

27. Ibid.; see also H.G. Birch and J.D. Gussow, *Disadvantaged Children: Health, Nutrition and School Failure* (New York: Harcourt, Brace and World, 1970), 319.

28. K. Warner Schaie, "Age Changes in Adult Intelligence," in *Aging: Scientific Perspectives and Social Issues*, ed. Diana S. Woodruff and James E. Birren (New York: D. Van Nostrand Co., 1975).

7

Why Advocates For the Elderly Have A Stake in Policies For Children

AN UNDERSTANDING of the common stake in intergenerational transfers leads to a broader view of the implications of policies directed at any one age group. Just as other age groups have a stake in policies directed at the elderly, so too do the elderly and their advocates have a stake—both moral and practical—in policies that affect the quality of life for other age groups.

As the previous chapter suggests, the practical stake of advocates for the elderly is grounded in two realities. First, since well-being in old age is partially a result of prior life events, advocates concerned about the quality of life for future cohorts of the elderly must be concerned with how social policies affect these cohorts at all points across the life course. Second, even those advocates who may be narrowly focused *only* on the interests of the current elderly (we hope their numbers are few) have a stake in policies directed at other age groups since the quality of life for the elderly is affected by the well-being of these other age groups.

While we do not intend to suggest here that the interests of all age groups and birth cohorts are identical and never conflict, we want to emphasize the stake advocates for the elderly have in policies directed at other age groups for several reasons. First, we believe it is important to show that far more holds the generations together than pulls them apart. An understanding of the interdependence and commonality of interests among generations could be lost amid the interest group competition engendered by a policy framework that frames issues in terms of conflict between generations. Second, such politics—whether engaged in by advocates of the elderly, of children, of baby boomers, or of other age-based interests—could be divisive and undermine the provision of public and private intergenerational transfers that respond to the needs of persons of all ages. Third, because this report is being written under the auspices of The Gerontological Society of America, an organization many identify as focused on research related to the elderly, we, as authors, feel a special obligation to underline the stake advocates for the elderly have in policies affecting other age groups. We do this not only to add to the credibility of our report, but also to emphasize our strong conviction that gerontology should be understood as *the study of aging across the life course* rather than as the study of the elderly exclusively.

Therefore, to illustrate the stake advocates for the elderly have in social policies affecting all age groups, this chapter discusses the special stake such advocates have in policies for children. We focus on the elderly and children because they are at different ends of the life course, a polarity that is frequently referenced when issues are framed in terms of competition and conflict between generations.

Clearly, the elderly and their advocates have strong moral reasons to support policies that respond to the needs of children. These reasons include the obligation of older generations to assist those who follow, and the fundamental right of all children to decent standards of living and to opportunities to fulfill their potential. In what follows, however, we focus on the practical reasons, among which we believe the most important to be:

- the economic interests of the elderly, now and in the future, in the productivity of future workers;

- the political interests of the elderly, now and in the future, 1) to maintain government as a mechanism that responds to need, and 2) to avoid intergenerational conflict; and

- the common interests of the elderly and children—especially the most vulnerable within these groups—in certain policy areas and issues.

ECONOMIC INTERESTS IN THE FUTURE
PRODUCTIVITY OF CHILDREN

Those concerned with meeting the needs of the elderly ought to help make sure that children get the family support and services necessary to enhance their future productivity as workers. As the Children's Defense Fund points out:

> investment in children is an intergenerational compact which protects our future security. Children need help during the eighteen years it takes to reach adulthood. But today's adults will later turn to these children for support during retirement years. In the future there will be more elderly people for the nation's economy to support. To protect ourselves in our old age, we must see to it that today's and tomorrow's children grow into productive and compassionate adults, because the security of all of us will come to rest on their shoulders.[1]

Unfortunately, the future productivity of a significant portion of children is being undermined by problems associated with poverty, changes in family structure, and uneven support for public education. Recent poverty trends provide one indication of the proportion of children at risk, as do data on health status, education, and the changing structure of the family.

During the last few years, for example, poverty rates among children under 18 have increased precipitously. Although they declined from about 26 percent to about 14 percent between 1959 and 1969 and then rose slightly in the 10 years that followed to nearly 16 percent in 1979, poverty rates among children increased very sharply in both the percent and number from 1979 through 1983,[2] primarily as a result of poor economic conditions and reductions in government spending. In 1984, when the official poverty threshold for a family of four was $10,609 and the near-poverty threshold was $13,261, more than one in five (21.3 percent) of all children under 18—that is, about 13.3 million out of the approximately 62 million children in the country—were officially defined as poor.[3] And roughly an additional 3.1 million children were hovering between the poverty threshold and the near-poverty threshold (125 percent of the poverty line).[4]

As with the elderly, the prevalence of poverty is not evenly distributed across all groups of children. While most poor children are white and not of Hispanic origin, nearly one-half of all black children

118

and two-fifths of all Hispanic children are poor compared with 15 percent of nonminority children.[5] Further, 55 percent of children living in single-parent households with female heads are poor.

Poverty-level incomes are not the only problems affecting so many of today's children. For example, the Children's Defense Fund reports the following:

- In 1982, "almost 200,000 babies were born to mothers who had late or no prenatal care," and such babies are three times more likely to have low birth weights, "the greatest single cause of death and birth defects" in the first year.[6]

- If current school dropout rates continue, "more than 6 million of the 41 million children now in school will not receive a high school diploma."[7]

- One in every six children are without health insurance, and they receive "only 75 percent of the care of children in the general population."[8]

- "Less than half of black preschool children are adequately immunized against diphtheria, pertussis, tetanus and polio," and one-third of all black children have never had dental care.[9]

Another concern of the Children's Defense Fund[10] and others[11] is what the changing family structure implies for the futures of children. For example, the House Select Committee on Children, Youth, and Families reports that 1) in 1982, 37 percent of children under 18 did not live in families where both biological parents were present, 2) the number of births out of wedlock between 1950 and 1980 increased fourfold to 666,000 (about 18 percent of all births), 3) divorce rates have more than doubled during the past 15 years to about 23 a year per 1000 married women, and 4) the number of female-headed families increased from less than 2 million in 1960 to nearly 6 million in 1983.[12] For many reasons, including the likelihood that children living in female-headed households will be poor or near poor, these trends suggest that changes in the structure of American families are placing the futures of increasing numbers of children at risk.

Implications for Future Cohorts of the Elderly

The baby boom cohort has a particular stake in the future productivity of children because today's children will constitute a substantial portion of the prime-age workers for most of the years during which the baby boomers are retired. Persons aged 18 and under in 1986 will be aged 24 to 42 when the first baby boomers begin to retire around 2010 and will be aged 44 to 62 at the height of baby boomer retirement in 2030.

No one can predict precisely what effect poverty and its correlates (e.g., less health care) among children will have on the productivity of the work force many years from now. It is certain, however, that the economic opportunities and potential productivity of a significant number of today's children are being constricted by poverty, limited access to health care, limited educational opportunities, and other problems. Further, the opportunities for a disproportionately large number of minority children—black, Native American, Hispanic, and Native and Pacific Islanders—are being similarly restricted. According to Martha Ozawa, professor of social policy at Washington University:

> Since nonwhite children will constitute an ever growing segment of the relatively shrinking child population, the optimal development of each nonwhite child will be crucial for creating future generations of productive workers. Because of demographic changes, the interests of nonwhite children and the interests of the elderly—especially the white elderly—will be interlocked. Informed white adults will have a vested interest in supporting public spending for nonwhite children so that their own old age will be secure.... At last the inevitability of mutual interdependence between the young and the old and, more pointedly, between nonwhite children and the white elderly can be seen—interdependence that means either the survival or decline of a satisfying quality of life for all.*[13]

Thus, the trends described by Samuel Preston (1985) and others[14] on the well-being of children—including increasing poverty, family instability, limited commitment to public education, and federal cutbacks (especially in programs serving poor children and their families)—should be very alarming to advocates for the elderly. This is so not simply for humanitarian reasons but also because the productivity of a grow-

---

*These observations about nonwhite children apply equally well to white Hispanic children and are also largely relevant to white children with limited opportunities.

ing portion of our future labor force may be undermined—with dire implications for the economy in general and for future cohorts of the elderly in particular.

POLITICAL INTERESTS IN CHILDREN'S POLICIES

Advocates for children and the elderly both have strong stakes in maintaining government as a responsive institution. Government at all levels has assumed substantial responsibility for helping meet many normal needs (e.g., education and retirement security) and some special needs (e.g., those originating from poverty or illness) of children and the elderly that individuals and families generally cannot meet entirely by themselves. Thus, while children receive relatively more assistance from their families and the elderly receive relatively more from government, both groups benefit directly from very substantial government programs.

Education is the key governmental service provided for children, with expenditures (mostly state and local) to school- and college-age children totaling about $142 billion (about 13 percent of all government expenditures) in fiscal year 1983.* Retirement income and health services are the major expenditures (predominately federal) directed at the elderly, with Social Security and Medicare expenditures—the direct benefits of which accrue primarily, but not entirely, to the elderly (see chap. 4)—totaling about $225 billion (about 20 percent of all government expenditures)[15] in fiscal year 1983.**

The safety net function of government is particularly important for the more vulnerable among children and the elderly. Without public intergenerational transfers, the life circumstances of those who are poor and/or unhealthy (or at greater risk of ill health) would be considerably worse. Altogether, local, state, and federal government expenditures for the major government programs directed at low-income elderly and children—Aid to Families with Dependent Children, Medicaid, Supplemental Security Income, public housing, Food Stamps, and nutrition programs—totaled about $86 billion (about 7.5 percent of all government expenditures) in fiscal year 1983.[16]***

---

*Figure includes $8.4 billion spent on vocational and adult education.

**Data from fiscal year 1983 are being used to facilitate comparisons between expenditures directed at young and old.

***Figure includes cost of general assistance, emergency assistance, and some social services.

It is plainly in the interest of the elderly to avoid, either in appearance or reality, intergenerational conflict. Activities on behalf of one narrowly defined, age-based interest in opposition to another—for instance, resistance from the elderly to increased taxation for schools, which would benefit children—would, if widespread, be self-defeating to the interests of both children and the elderly. Such activities would serve to define the elderly and their supporters as special interests with little concern for the needs of other groups, thereby distracting attention from the common stake all age groups have in policies addressed to human need.

Again, this is not to suggest either that the elderly's interests are identical to those of children or that their interests never conflict. Indeed, their interests *do* occasionally differ and sometimes even conflict, particularly over short-run allocations of resources. In the long run, however, the elderly as a group and their supporters have much more to gain by supporting children's policies and programs. Ultimately, society's concern for the elderly emerges from a more generalized concern with the common welfare. Thus, it is to their advantage that advocates for the elderly recognize this and support the claims of other groups consistent with this concern. Failure to do so could lead to the unraveling of many policies that benefit persons of all ages.

COMMON INTERESTS OF ADVOCATES
FOR THE ELDERLY AND CHILDREN

Finally, the advocates for the elderly have a stake in policies directed at children because children and the elderly—especially the most vulnerable among them—have several needs in common, including

- adequate income,

- adequate health care,

- adequate, publicly funded personal social services,

- dignity when receiving public services and benefits,

- productive roles in society, and

- policies that support the care-giving functions of the family.

Need for Adequate Income

Both children and the elderly (and their advocates) have a mutual interest in the promotion of adequate income maintenance policies. Programs like Social Security and Unemployment Insurance provide partial protection to nearly all households against loss of income due to retirement, disability, death of a wage earner, or unemployment. As previously shown, over the long run and even at any given moment in time, children and the elderly benefit both directly and indirectly from these programs (see chap. 4). For instance, while the elderly are the major beneficiaries of Social Security at any given time, currently about 3.3 million children also receive Social Security benefits each month. Further, the households of nearly all other children are partially protected from loss of income due to disability or death of a wage earner, and over the long run the vast majority of today's children will eventually become beneficiaries of Social Security.

Similarly, the approximately 13.3 million children under age 18 and 3.3 million elderly persons officially defined as poor in 1984, and the approximately 5.5 million children and elderly hovering just above the poverty level,[17] have a common stake in maintaining and improving the adequacy of public assistance programs such as Aid to Families with Dependent Children, Supplemental Security Income, and Food Stamps, as well as a shared interest in tax policies that are advantageous for low-income persons. The federal tax code, for example, provides an exemption for each child and also permits the elderly to take two exemptions instead of just the one provided to persons under 65. However, because low-income persons pay very little or no taxes at all, these exemptions are of negligible value to low-income children and elderly. In fact, higher-income persons benefit the most from them, while low-income children and elderly could actually benefit far more from other arrangements.

Need for Adequate Health Care

Children and the elderly also share a concern in promoting policies that provide access to high-quality health care. In addition to their common interest in maintaining and improving programs such as Medicaid, Medicare, veteran's health programs, maternal and child health programs, and immunization, they are also affected by policies that promote expansion of private health insurance coverage and effective cost containment measures.

Need for Adequate, Publicly Funded Personal Social Services

Children and the elderly both need adequate, publicly funded personal social services. Despite some overlap, such social services are distinct from the other five social welfare services: income maintenance, health, education, employment, and housing. The major functions of the personal social services* are 1) to facilitate access to social welfare programs in general (e.g., through legal services, case advocacy, hotlines); 2) to treat and control individuals and their personal problems and/or deviant behavior (e.g., through individual and group counseling, child and adult protective services, homemakers); and 3) to enhance human growth and development (e.g., through senior citizen centers, certain summer camp programs, family life education).[18]

These services are mainly provided by departments of social services located in hundreds of counties around the country, although many personal social services are part of other systems such as hospitals, schools, and courts. Additionally, these services are provided by other public agencies (e.g., senior citizen centers) and through both private social service agencies (e.g., family service agencies) and occasionally private individuals (e.g., family day care) who contract with public agencies to deliver personal social services.[19]

The extent to which age or financial need should determine eligibility for personal social services is under debate. Some argue that a family-oriented personal social service system that is age-neutral would be preferable. Others believe that a system in which eligibility is only sometimes age- and/or income-related allows for more flexibility in targeting services to populations with special needs.

Regardless, it is clearly in the interest of children and the elderly to have access to viable public social services that assist in preventing or ameliorating personal problems and in enhancing overall quality of life.

---

*For children and their families, the major funding sources of these services are 1) Title XX of the Social Security Act—now called the Social Service Block Grant—which funds services (e.g., day care, information and referral, protective services for abused and neglected children, foster care, adoption, homemakers, and counseling) that are primarily, but not exclusively, for low-income children; 2) Title IVB of the Social Security Act, which funds the traditional child welfare services (e.g., foster care and adoption); and 3) Title IVE of the Social Security Act, which provides financial participation to state foster care and adoption programs.

For the elderly, the major funding sources are 1) The Older Americans Act, which funds a variety of programs and services (e.g., multipurpose senior citizen centers, information and referral, congregate meals, meals on wheels, planning and advocacy efforts, transportation, and opportunities to participate in part-time community service jobs) that are primarily for persons aged 60 and over, and 2) Title XX of the Social Security Act, which funds services (e.g., homemakers, transportation to medical appointments, case management for disabled elderly, meals on wheels, protective services for abused and neglected adults, and information and referral) that are primarily, but not exclusively, for low-income elderly.

Need for Dignity When Receiving Public Services and Benefits

Although obvious, it is worth noting that children and the elderly have a strong interest in being treated with dignity when receiving services and benefits to which they are entitled. Without belaboring the point, its importance as a factor affecting the self-respect and quality of life for beneficiaries should not be underestimated.

Need for Productive Roles in Society

Productive behavior takes many forms and continues throughout the life course, though the mix changes as individuals age.[20] This observation is especially important in a society in which individuals have generally been spending more time in retirement and educational pursuits. Thus, it is essential that society provide opportunities for children and the elderly to engage in and receive recognition for such productive albeit nonincome-producing activities.

Children and the elderly especially benefit from social policies that encourage activities such as voluntary or part-time employment in nonprofessional human service positions and participation in informal education. Further, programs that increase intergenerational contact provide productive activity that is particularly in the interest of young and old—for example, programs that encourage the elderly to volunteer in elementary and/or secondary schools and programs that either encourage young and old to learn together or encourage the young to teach the old.[21] Involvement in such activities often serves the dual purpose of providing a needed service while increasing the sense of efficacy and general well-being of the person performing it.

Need for Policies That Support the Care-Giving Functions of the Family

As emphasized in chapter 3, the family is generally both the preferred and major provider of care to its members. All children and elderly—indeed, all generations—therefore share a common stake in social policies that support and enhance the family's ability to provide care to its members. This concern can be illustrated by the growing need for community-based long-term care primarily for the elderly and by the growing need for child care services.

As regards the elderly, the convergence of trends (e.g., the expanding population of the very old and changes in family composition) is increasing the need for community-based long-term care services—including case management, homemaker-home health aides, visiting nurses, and transportation—for functionally disabled elders.

The House Select Committee on Children, Youth, and Families

has pointed out parallel growth in the demand for child care services—that is, in the need for day care for preschoolers and infants and for after-school care for older children. The trends contributing to this growth are "the anticipated increase in the proportion of children living with only one parent" combined with the increases in female labor force participation—especially among single mothers and mothers with preschoolers. For example, the population under age 6 living with single mothers is projected to increase from about 6 million in 1980 to 8.9 million in 1990. Further, 63 percent of single mothers with children under 6 are projected to be in the labor force in 1990, as are 55 percent of mothers with children under 6 in households where the father is present.[22]

Not only are demographic and population trends accelerating a demand for more community-based long-term care and child care services, but these service needs have other similarities. Children and the elderly stand to benefit from policies that 1) expand the range of available care options; 2) assure quality care through proper regulation of service providers; 3) protect and expand sources of funding for these services; and 4) assist family members who often wish to, and must, provide care to children and the elderly while also engaging in paid employment and meeting the needs of others in their households.

SUMMARY AND CONCLUSIONS

The special stake advocates for the elderly have in children's policies is a telling illustration of the interest that such advocates have in social policies affecting the well-being of *all* nonelderly age groups:

- Future cohorts of the elderly will benefit from policies that maintain and enhance the productivity of future labor forces.

- The elderly have a political interest in pursuing a strategy that both maintains government as a mechanism responsive to need and avoids intergenerational conflict.

- The elderly have common interests with other age groups both in maintaining and developing particular policies and in resolving common problems.

Further, those advocates concerned with future as well as current cohorts of the elderly must consider how the quality of life for these future cohorts is shaped by social policies at all points across their lives.

We would be remiss, too, if we did not point out that advocates for the elderly have an obligation to be concerned with more than just the current elderly, an obligation that arises both from the very special relationship the elderly have to the future and from their unique role as conveyors of culture.

Because some elderly—we suspect many—are concerned with the kind of future their children and grandchildren will have, advocates for the elderly have a responsibility to be similarly concerned. It is estimated that 80 percent of the elderly have at least one living child, that 38 percent are part of three-generation families, and that 36 percent are part of four-generation families.[23] Although obvious, it is worth noting that those elderly who are concerned with their children, grandchildren, and great-grandchildren must also be concerned with the well-being of the people around their progeny. This concern points up still another reason for advocates for the elderly to support policies and programs that improve the quality of life for young adults and the middle-aged.

Finally, some elderly—and again we believe there are many—take pleasure in contributing to a legacy of social progress. For them, continuing this contribution to family, friends, and society and supporting policies and programs that improve the quality of life for those who follow is an important part of that legacy.

Notes

1. Children's Defense Fund, *A Children's Defense Fund Budget: An Analysis of the President's FY 1986 Budget and Children* (Washington, D.C., 1985), 71.

2. Congressional Budget Office (hereafter referred to as CBO), *Reducing Poverty Among Children* (Washington, D.C.: U.S. GPO, 1985), 5.

3. Bureau of the Census, "Money Income and Poverty Status: 1984."

4. Ibid.

5. CBO, *Reducing Poverty Among Children*, 6.

6. Children's Defense Fund, *A Children's Defense Fund Budget*, 7.

7. Ibid., 36.

8. Ibid., 31.

9. Ibid.

10. Ibid., 1-50.

11. Samuel H. Preston, "Children and the Elderly in the U.S.," *Scientific American* 251, no. 6 (n.d.): 44-49; Daniel Patrick Moynihan, "Family and Nation," Godkin Lectures, Harvard University, Cambridge, Mass., 8-9 November 1985; House Select Committee on Children, Youth, and Families, *Children, Youth, and Families: 1983 A Year-End Report*, 98th Cong., 2d sess., March 1984, Committee Print, 96-97.

12. House Select Committee on Children, Youth, and Families, *Children, Youth, and Families: 1983*, 96, 97.

13. Martha Ozawa, "Non-Whites and the Demographic Imperative in Social Welfare Spending" (Paper presented at the 1985 National Association of Social Work Professional Symposium, Chicago, Ill., 8 November 1985, Mimeographed).

14. Preston, "Children and the Elderly in the U.S."; Children's Defense Fund, *A Children's Defense Fund Budget*; CBO, *Reducing Poverty Among Children*; Ozawa, "Non-Whites and the Demographic Imperative."

15. Ann Kallman Bixby, "Social Welfare Expenditures under Public Welfare Programs, Fiscal Year 1983," *Social Security Bulletin* (forthcoming).

16. Ibid.

17. Bureau of the Census, "Money Income and Poverty Status: 1984."

18. Donald Fandetti, associate professor, University of Maryland School of Social Work and Community Planning, personal communication, Baltimore, Md., 16 June 1985.

19. Ibid.

20. Robert Kahn, "Productive Behavior Through the Life Course," in *Policy Implications of an Aging Population* (Washington, D.C.: Consortium of Social Science Associations, 1985), 17-20.

21. Ira Mothner, *Children and Others: Intergenerational Relations in an Aging Society*, from a conference co-sponsored by the Aging Society Project of the Carnegie Corporation of New York and the Foundation for Child Development (New York: Carnegie Corporation of New York, 1985).

22. House Select Committee on Children, Youth, and Families, *Demographic and Social Trends: Implications for Federal Support of Dependent-Care Services for Children and the Elderly*, 98th Cong., 1st sess., December 1983, Committee Print, iv.

23. Ethel Shanas, "Older People and Their Families," *Journal of Marriage and the Family* 42, no. 1 (n.d.): 9-15.

8

Intergenerational Inequity: Why It Won't Work As a Framework for Policy

EARLIER we mentioned that the tone and character of the debate being generated by a loosely defined concept of intergenerational inequity prompted the decision to prepare this report. Following that, we put forth our view about why, in an interdependent and aging society, all generations have a common stake in intergenerational transfers that assist families and individuals in responding to needs existing at all points across the life course. Here we caution about the pitfalls of using inter-generational inequity[1]—a concept based on a narrow view of equity between generations—as the basis for policy.

In doing so, we recognize that there is room for disagreement and that there are well-informed and well-motivated persons who have reached other conclusions. We also recognize that, while we disgree with some about framing policy questions in terms of competition and conflict between generations, we often agree about the need to address concerns such as the high rate of poverty among children, to reduce large federal government and international trade deficits, to prepare for the retirement of the baby boomers, and to encourage economic growth. Although we are critical of the concept of intergenerational inequity and particularly deplore its use in the policy-making process, we are *not* opposing the goal of fairness, either in society or between genera-tions. We are simply concerned that applying a narrow understanding of equity between generations to the policy process may have unex-pected and undesirable consequences.

Briefly stated, this is the rationale of the intergenerational inequity approach, as we understand it:

Due to previous circumstances of the elderly and the broad-based perceptions of the elderly as both "needy" and "worthy," there has been a flow of public resources (income, health, and social services) toward the elderly, which has successfully improved their economic status and access to health care. In fact, the elderly are (or shortly will be) financially better off than the nonaged population. In light of this improved status, of large federal deficits, of the cost to younger persons of continuing present policies, and of the anticipated growth of the elderly population, the flow of resources to the elderly seems "intergenerationally inequitable" and a source of intergenerational conflict.

Emerging as a catch-all slogan for a number of concerns, complaints, and/or calls for policy changes, the intergenerational inequity argument reflects beliefs such as the following:

• Programs for the elderly are a major cause of current budget deficits and economic problems.

• The elderly receive too large a portion of public social welfare expenditures to the detriment of children and other groups.

• Because of demographic trends, the future costs of programs for the elderly will place an intolerable burden on future cohorts of younger workers.

• Younger people will not receive fair returns on their Social Security and Medicare investments.

While the concerns and charges may vary, the constant implication running through each is that policies and programs for the elderly are "unfair" and lead to intergenerational conflict. For example, in a futuristic political novel by Colorado's Governor Richard D. Lamm, a committee in the year 2000 sends the president of the United States a warning memorandum on intergenerational conflict:

Simply put, America's elderly have become an intolerable burden on the economic system and the younger generation's future. In the name of compassion for the elderly, we have handcuffed the young, mortgaged their future, and drastically limited their hopes and aspirations.

The policymakers of the 1960s and 1970s . . . . set up unsustainable pension systems. . . . They placed the bill for all these programs on succeeding generations, who consequently inherited the crippled economy their excesses caused. . . . The biblical story of the prodigal son has been turned on its head: we now have the sad but true story of the "prodigal father."[2]

Besides being a slogan, intergenerational inequity, as used in the policy-making process, 1) frames policy issues in terms of competition and conflict between young and old over the distribution of resources; 2) uses a narrow understanding of "fairness" and narrow measures of transfers of selected resources between generations to determine the fairness of public policy; and 3) incorporates a point of view that leads to particular policy goals and prescriptions. This framework, if accepted, can set the terms of debate, not only over policies for the elderly but also over other social policies concerned with needs occurring throughout life. But certainly our society should be concerned about the well-being of people at all points in the life course, and certainly intergenerational conflict should be avoided. Thus, it is important to assess the actual or implied assumptions this framework creates for evaluating and making policy.

Our examination of this approach to policy-making identifies several serious flaws. These include

• misunderstandings about the common stake persons of all ages have in policies directed primarily at the elderly (as well as in policies directed primarily at other groups);

• misunderstandings about the diversity of elderly and nonelderly populations;

• misunderstandings about the implications of the changing composition of the age structure of society;

• the use of narrow concepts of fairness;

• the fact that equity between generations is a notion virtually impossible to measure accurately; and

* a misunderstanding of relations between generations which, oddly enough, may *promote* intergenerational conflict and distract attention—somewhat like a red herring—away from important social issues.

MISUNDERSTANDINGS ABOUT THE COMMON STAKE IN POLICIES FOR THE ELDERLY

As presented within the intergenerational inequity framework, public programs for the elderly benefit only the elderly. This view chiefly results from 1) defining issues in terms of competition between generations over scarce resources; 2) looking at the flow of benefits from programs like Social Security and Medicare at only one point in time (cross-sectionally) rather than over time (longitudinally); and 3) ignoring some direct and many indirect benefits that go to nonelderly persons.

For example, to support an argument calling for reductions in Social Security benefits, a 5 November 1984 editorial in *U.S. News and World Report* argues that today's Social Security system "is nothing less than a massive transfer of wealth from the young, many of them struggling, to the elderly, many living comfortably."[3]

With increasing regularity, the press and popular commentators refer to the amount of the federal budget that "goes" to the elderly as if only the elderly benefit from these programs. While a cross-sectional view of the federal budget does suggest that about 28 percent of federal expenditures are for programs whose direct benefits are primarily for the elderly, to conclude that these expenditures benefit *only* the elderly assumes that the elderly do not pay or have never paid taxes and that nonelderly persons do not benefit in any way from the resources that flow to the elderly. But the elderly *do* pay federal taxes—an estimated $36 billion in federal income taxes in 1982, or about 13 percent of all personal federal income taxes collected in that year;[4] moreover, some younger persons *do* receive direct benefits (see chap. 4) from programs "for" the elderly (e.g., survivors benefits in Social Security). In the same way, the elderly, like everyone else, benefit in many ways from other federal expenditures (e.g., highway construction, national defense, etc.).

A long-term perspective shows further that over time benefits from policies directed principally at the elderly represent flows of resources among different cohorts (see chaps. 1 and 4). For example, from a longitudinal viewpoint, current workers will eventually be direct beneficiaries of Social Security and Medicare, programs into which current elderly beneficiaries or their spouses have already contributed through both payroll taxes and their investments in the perpetuation and growth of society. Thus, the long-term perspective suggests persons of all ages have a common stake in these programs:

• Younger persons benefit indirectly since, for example, Social Security stimulates "investments in the families of children, by freeing grown children of the need to support their elders" and by reducing the amount of savings the middle-aged need for their own retirement.[5]

• Younger persons benefit indirectly since most funds transferred to the elderly quickly circulate back through the economy.

• Families benefit indirectly since these programs reduce intrafamily tensions and generally enhance the dignity of family members who receive benefits.

The intergenerational inequity framework is also based on, and promotes similar misunderstandings about, who benefits from programs directed at *other* age groups. It implies, for example, that only children benefit from programs designed primarily to respond to their needs. This, too, is not true, as we show elsewhere in the report by identifying the common stake persons of all ages have both in policies for children (see chap. 7) and in policies that assist families in their many care-giving activities (see chap. 3). As often applied to policy discussions, the intergenerational inequity framework is based on a limited understanding of who benefits from social policies, thereby resulting in a misunderstanding about the many intergenerational implications of such policies, ranging from those directed primarily at the elderly to those directed primarily at children.

MISUNDERSTANDINGS ABOUT THE DIVERSITY OF THE ELDERLY

The traditional stereotype of the elderly as a homogeneous population that is weak, ill, and poor is being replaced by a new stereotype of an equally homogeneous population—that of a well-off special interest group whose very success in gaining entitlements may place an unfair burden on the work force, especially as their numbers increase.[6] The intergenerational inequity framework draws heavily on this new stereotype.

Misunderstandings About the Economic Status of the Elderly

Take, for example, the economic status of the elderly. Boston College economist Joseph Quinn writes:

> never begin a sentence with "The elderly are . . ." or "The elderly do. . . ." No matter what you are discussing, some are, and some are not; some do, and some do not. The most important characteristic about the aged is their diversity. The least interesting summary statistic is the average, because it ignores the tremendous dispersion around it. Beware of the mean.[7]

Nevertheless, the press and some analysts and policymakers increasingly fall into the trap of overlooking this heterogeneity in declaring how the economic status of the elderly has improved. Writing in the 18 February 1980 issue of *Forbes* magazine, Jerry Flint notes:

> The myth is that they're sunk in poverty. The reality is that they're living well. The trouble is that there are too many of them—God bless 'em.[8]

Recently, the Council of Economic Advisors, in its 1985 *Annual Report*, devoted a chapter to the economic status of the elderly, which emphasizes that

> the income of the elderly has increased faster over the past two decades than the income of the non-elderly population. Today, elderly and non-elderly families have about equal levels of income per capita. Poverty rates among the elderly have declined so dramatically that in 1983 poverty rates for the elderly were lower than poverty rates for the rest of the population.[9]

These findings were widely circulated through the media, sometimes as part of editorial comments suggesting that perhaps we have gone "a bit too far" in meeting the elderly's income needs. That they provide a rather homogeneous view of the elderly, that the elderly's average income started from a very low base 20 years ago, and that these conclusions are based on some questionable statistics was not reported, however. Mean per capita income (before taxes) is a weak measure to use when comparing the income of elderly households—usually consisting of one or two persons—with that of nonelderly households. For example, the standard of living for a family of four with per capita incomes of $7,500—a total household income of $30,000—is likely to be superior to that of an elderly individual living alone whose money income is $7,500. Moreover, since there are a disproportionately large number of elderly households (compared with nonelderly households) of substantial wealth, a measure based on the mean tends to overstate the income position of the ''typical'' elderly household and hide the diversity of circumstances among the elderly. In fact, while the poverty incidence for the elderly is less than that for the rest of the population, it is larger than that for other adult age groups. That some of these points and others related to the heterogeneity of the elderly are noted but not emphasized, both in the Council of Economic Advisors study and in some other recent studies examining the improved economic status of the elderly,[10] plays into the media's tendency to simplify complex matters and report that the elderly are doing better than the nonelderly.

Unfortunately, stereotyping the elderly's economic status leads many to overlook the type of balanced assessment made by economist Marilyn Moon when she was with the Urban Institute. Pointing out that there is both good news and bad news about the economic status of the elderly, Moon notes that while

> the good news should not deflect attention from the problems that remain, it is not a sign of callousness or lack of concern to admit that there have been achievements in this area. Nor does this imply necessarily that the elderly are doing so well that government aid should be cut. *In fact, part of the significance of the ''good'' news is that it underscores the importance of government transfers in achieving gains.* [Emphasis added][11]

Examples of the Economic Diversity of the Elderly

While the median income for families headed by persons 65 and over in 1984 was $18,236, and $7,349 for unrelated individuals 65 and over, it is the diversity around these averages that is most striking (see chart 8.1). Almost one-fifth of these families reported incomes under $10,000 while approximately one-quarter reported incomes of $30,000 and over. Further, 25 percent of elderly individuals reported incomes under $5,000 while 11 percent reported incomes over $20,000.[12]

The failure to recognize economic diversity among the elderly also encourages many to overlook the substantial pockets of poverty that

Chart 8.1
Diversity of Incomes Among Elderly Families
and Individuals in 1984

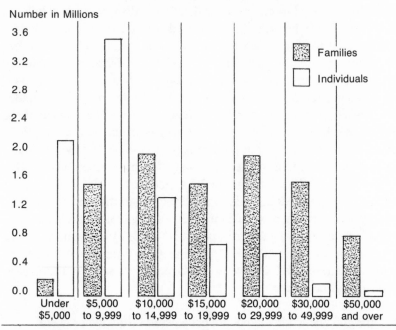

Number in Millions

| | Families |
| | Individuals |

Source: Bureau of the Census, "Money Income and Poverty Status of Families and Persons in the United States: 1984" (advance data from the March 1985 *Current Population Survey*), *Current Population Reports*, ser. P-60, no. 149 (Washington, D.C.: U.S. GPO, August 1985).

still exist. For example, 32 percent of elderly blacks, 22 percent of elderly Hispanics, 20 percent of elderly whites living in female-headed households, and an astonishing 57 percent of elderly black women living alone are included among the 12.4 percent of the elderly defined as poor in 1984.[13]*

Further, there are what University of Utah economist Timothy Smeeding terms "the Tweeners." These are largely lower middle-income elderly households whose incomes are between the poverty line and two times the poverty line, but not large enough to protect them from economic insecurity related to inadequate health insurance protection, high housing costs, or dependence on Social Security as their

---

*In 1984, the poverty threshold for an elderly individual was $4,979 and for an elderly couple, $6,282.

primary income source.[14] While plainly not poor by a money income definition of poverty, this group has very limited ability to absorb expenses such as those related to chronic illness.

Implications of Stereotypic Thinking

The intergenerational inequity framework draws on and promotes this new stereotype of the elderly as a well-off special interest group and as overconsumers of health care. Failure to recognize the heterogeneity existing among them—even among those aged 85 and over—leads to distortions in how social problems are defined and limits the types of policy options given serious consideration. Unfortunately, these stereotypes persist, in part because stereotypical thinking is convenient, in part because negative attitudes toward the elderly and growing old persist, and in part because such stereotyping furthers certain political ends such as reducing social programs. Failure to recognize the heterogeneity existing among the elderly also distracts attention from their many current and potential contributions, ranging from continued employment to community and family participation.

MISUNDERSTANDINGS ABOUT THE IMPLICATIONS OF POPULATION AGING

Anticipated changes in the size and significance of the elderly population are substantial. As noted previously, the Census Bureau projects 1) a doubling of the number of people aged 65 and over by 2030; 2) an increase in the percent of the population that is elderly, from about 12 percent in 1985 to 21.2 percent in 2030; and 3) large increases in the number of persons aged 85 and over—the very old—from 2.7 million in 1985 to 4.9 million in 2000, 8.6 million in 2030, and 16 million in 2050[15]* (see chap.2).

Unfortunately, recognition of these trends is often accompanied by undue pessimism about our society's ability to meet the needs of future generations of the elderly.

The intergenerational inequity framework carries the belief that, as a result of population aging, future costs of programs for the elderly

---

*The projected increase in the proportion of the population aged 65 and over is primarily due to the assumed leveling-off of birth rates combined with the aging of current cohorts, especially the baby boomers.[16] Anticipated improvements in old age mortality play a secondary, though important, role in this trend. The projected increase in numbers is primarily due to the aging of the baby boomers and secondarily due to anticipated increases in life expectancy at age 65.

will place an intolerable burden on future cohorts of younger workers. Arguing for cuts in the Social Security COLA and suggesting introduction of a means test, an editorial in the 5 November 1984 *U.S. News and World Report* suggests that the payroll tax can only get worse, noting that today, "3 workers support 1 pensioner. By 2035 it will be 2 to 1."[17]* Similarly, Phillip Longman maintains in the June 1985 *Atlantic Monthly* that unless "many fundamental trends are soon reversed, the Baby Boomers are headed for a disastrous retirement."[18]

While not necessarily concluding that commitments to government services ought to be reduced, some analysts question whether current levels of effort can be sustained in the future by a smaller working-age population. In an article entitled "Guns vs. Canes," Barbara Boyle Torrey summarizes three studies, which project that the share of the federal budget going to the elderly will increase from 25 percent in 1980 to between 46 percent and 51 percent in 2025, when it is assumed that the overall federal budget will be 20 percent of GNP. She also summarizes a fourth study, which (using different assumptions about constraints on the growth of the federal budget) projects that 41.5 percent of the federal budget will go to the elderly.[19]

Three Fundamental Flaws

These predictions sound ominous indeed, but the implications of population aging are not so worrisome. No doubt the population is aging, and no doubt this will require changes in how we respond to human needs. It is reasonable to assume, for example, that demand for health services and the like will be greater and that pressures on public and private pensions will increase. But the demographic determinism implicit in the intergenerational inequity framework relies on three misunderstandings about the implications of population aging and thus cannot replace careful consideration of the problems before us.

The "aged dependency ratio" is misleading. First, take the oft-referenced "aged dependency ratio" (also called the "elderly support ratio")—that is, the number of persons aged 65 and over (and, for the purpose of the measure, presumed "dependent") for every 100 persons aged 18 to 64 (presumed to be "contributing to the economy"). The number of dependent persons aged 65 and over per 100 "nondependent" persons has increased—from 15.2 persons in 1955 to 18.8 persons in 1982, and it is projected to rise slowly to 21.9 persons in 2010

---

*The use of the term *pensioner* is incorrect here. The correct term would be *beneficiary*, which includes persons receiving Social Security disability and survivors benefits as well as retirement benefits.

(see table 8.1 and chart 8.2). After that, very precipitous increases are projected with the aging of the baby boomers, so that the ratio is expected to double to 37.0 persons[20] by 2030.

This aged dependency ratio, however, only shows part of the "dependency burden." In contrast, the "overall dependency ratio" (also called the "total support ratio") measures the total number of persons under 18 plus those aged 65 and over for every 100 persons aged 18 through 64. From 1985 through 2010, the overall dependency ratio is projected to be quite stable (varying between 63.7 and 58.1), actually reaching its lowest point around 2010 (58.1). Even in 2030—at the height of baby boomer retirement—the overall dependency ratio (74.8) is projected to be well below that during the 1960s (when the great majority of baby boomers were under 18) (see table 8.1 and chart 8.2). In fact, since the proportion of the population under 18 is projected to decline,

Table 8.1
Number of Dependents per 100 Persons
Aged 18 to 64 Years, 1950–2080*

Year	Total	Under age 18	Age 65 years and over
Estimates			
1950	64.4	51.0	13.3
1955	73.5	58.3	15.2
1960	81.6	64.9	16.8
1965	83.1	65.7	17.4
1970	78.0	60.6	17.5
1975	71.3	53.3	18.0
1980	64.6	46.0	18.6
1982	62.9	44.1	18.8
Projections			
1985	62.1	42.7	19.4
1990	62.5	41.9	20.6
1995	63.7	42.3	21.4
2000	61.8	40.7	21.1
2010	58.1	36.2	21.9
2020	65.6	36.9	28.7
2030	74.8	37.8	37.0
2050	74.6	36.6	38.0
2080	78.1	36.2	41.9

*Projection data from middle series. As of July 1. Includes Armed Forces Overseas.

Source: Bureau of the Census, "Projections of the Population of the United States, by Age, Sex, and Race: 1983–2080," *Current Population Reports*, ser. P-25, no. 952 (Washington, D.C.: U.S. GPO, 1984).

Chart 8.2
Overall Dependency Ratio
Number of Children and Aged
Per 100 Adults, 18-64: 1940-2040

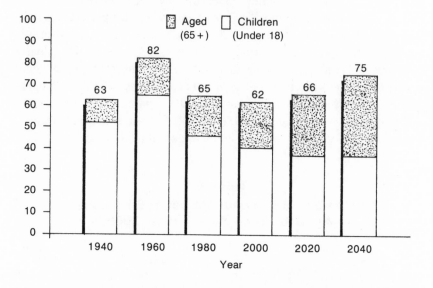

Source: Bureau of the Census, "Projections of the Population of the United States, by Age, Sex, and Race: 1983–2080," *Current Population Reports*, ser. P-25, no. 952, middle series (Washington, D.C.: U.S. GPO, 1984).

Torrey points out that *never at any time during the next 65 years is the overall dependency ratio projected to exceed the levels it attained in 1964*.[21] While the composition of governmental and private expenditures for younger and older Americans is quite different, the dependency ratio does not support such a gloomy view of society's ability, through public and private mechanisms, to enhance the quality of life for all.

Further, as Brandeis University researcher William Crown notes, both the aged dependency ratio and the overall dependency ratio are flawed indicators of the economy's ability to support an aging population, and they lead to unduly pessimistic conclusions. The latter may be somewhat the better of the two, but it too has methodological problems. Neither ratio takes into account 1) the current contributions of those elderly (or persons under age 18) who are employed; 2) the potential for increased labor force participation among the elderly; or 3) the recent change in the Social Security Act, which gradually increases the age of eligibility for full retirement benefits from 65 to 67 over a 27-year period beginning in 2000—a change that will result in a more favorable ratio of workers to nonworkers than what is projected by the aged and overall dependency ratios. As Crown points out, studies that account for the differing labor force participation rates of various age/sex groups (for example, the growth in the number of working women) predict less of a total burden of population aging on the labor force than that experienced in recent decades.[22]

Dependency ratios also do not consider the effect of a growing economy. Crown shows that if the economy expands at 2 percent each year—a relatively modest rate of expansion by historical standards—"the real costs of supporting each dependent person in 2050 could be 5.6 times higher than in 1960 without any increased burden to society."[23] In other words, even if the per capita costs of sustaining future dependents are much greater than they are today, economic growth will enable our society to afford the additional costs.

It is important to assess the implications of changing dependency ratios within the context of an expanding economy. Using the most commonly accepted midrange assumptions of the Social Security Administration (Alternative IIB) about economic growth and the size of the future U.S. population, real GNP per person is expected to nearly double by 2020 and triple by 2050* (see table 8.2). Even if the economy performs more sluggishly over the long run than the Social Security Administration projects, it is extremely likely that there will be considerably more goods and services produced per American. Undoubtedly, there are numerous distributional issues; for example, if the percent of GNP directed at the nonworking population increases, future workers would quite probably pay relatively higher taxes. Of most importance, these data show that, barring unforeseen disasters such as nuclear war, the economy of the future can in all likelihood support all age groups at a standard of living that is better, on average, than that prevailing today.

Reductions in public expenditures have private costs. The second problem with the demographic determinism inherent in the intergenerational inequity framework is that, in suggesting public expenditures for the elderly should be reduced, it ignores the fact that one way or another—either by government, family, or individual effort—society *will* respond to the most salient needs of the elderly. Reductions in

---

*Real GNP per person (or real per capita gross national product) refers to the inflation-adjusted value of all goods and services produced over a year in the American economy divided by the number of persons in the U.S. population.

Table 8.2
Past and Estimated GNP Per Person[a]
(After Adjusting for Inflation)
for the U.S. Population

Year	Estimated Real GNP (in billions of dollars)[b]	Past and Projected Total U.S. Population (millions)[c]	Estimated Real GNP Per Person (in 1972 dollars)
1960	737	189	3,900
1970	1,086	214	5,070
1980	1,475	236	6,250
1990	1,943	258	7,520
2000	2,498	277	9,010
2010	3,108	294	10,580
2020	3,687	308	11,980
2030	4,355	317	13,720
2040	5,207	323	16,110
2050	6,229	327	19,060
2060	7,496	331	22,670

[a] Based on intermediate (Alternative IIB) assumptions as used in the *1985 Annual Report of the Social Security Board of Trustees.*

[b] Estimates are in 1972 dollars.

[c] Includes estimates for the United States and for persons outside the 50 states and the District of Columbia who are covered by Social Security.

government effort would simply shift many costs to individuals and families. But while individual savings should be encouraged and families should and do provide care to disabled elderly members (see chap. 3), shifting *too many* costs could have negative and unanticipated side effects. Such reductions might, for example, result in increased pressure on younger persons to cut investments in their children (or have fewer children) either to save for their old age or to respond to the financial and/or health care needs of elderly family members. They could also result in greater reliance on welfare—with a corresponding loss of dignity—among those elderly who lack families or whose families cannot afford to meet their needs. In short, the needs of a growing elderly population will not go away, no matter what is done to governmental programs. Both private and public efforts are necessary to respond to these needs. Consequently, the real issue concerns the proper mix of individual effort, family assistance, and government services.

The future can be shaped. The third problem with this view of the demography of aging is that it assumes that the future is immutable:

that population aging will inevitably result in an intolerable burden on future workers unless commitments provided through social programs are significantly reduced.

This view of the future is unduly pessimistic. First, it assumes what most analysts consider unlikely—namely, that the economy will not grow. But, more importantly, it assumes that policymakers have no choice but to accept passively a particular vision of the future—one in which, for example, a large portion of the GNP is consumed to provide health care to a large elderly population, especially the very old.

But policymakers have a variety of tools at their disposal, which, while not enabling them to control the future, can at least help shape it. Monetary and fiscal decisions can significantly affect the economy of the future. Workers can be encouraged or discouraged to stay in the labor force past what are today considered the early and normal retirement ages. Changes are already scheduled in Social Security—including liberalizations of the delayed retirement credit and the earnings test, and the gradual increase in the eligibility age for full retirement benefits—that will encourage increased work effort among the elderly. Tax policies that encourage firms to offer early and very early retirement options in their private pension plans could also be changed, and several incentives could be developed to encourage private employers to offer part-time employment opportunities to elderly workers. Moreover, encouraging research for prevention and treatment of chronic conditions such as Alzheimer's disease, other dementing illnesses, osteoporosis, osteoarthritis, and urinary incontinence is likely both to reduce the anticipated rate of increase in future public and private expenditures needed to treat these debilitating conditions and to improve the quality of life for the children, young, and middle-aged workers of today who will be tomorrow's elderly.

NARROW CONCEPTS OF FAIRNESS

The view of social justice promoted by the intergenerational inequity framework is extremely narrow and therefore misleading, for four reasons:

1. *Equity between generations is a very limited criterion by which to judge the social justice (fairness) of distributing scarce resources among those with competing claims.* Even if we could agree on what constitutes a fair distribution of resources among generations and achieve such a balance, there is no reason to believe that this definition of social justice would conform with more than a small minority of citizens' views

of how society ought to distribute scarce resources. Achieving such a fair distribution between generations does not guarantee social justice in ways that are crucial to many citizens and policymakers. It does not guarantee 1) that poor citizens will be provided with minimally adequate resources; 2) that nonpoor citizens will be protected from the risks of drastic reduction in their standard of living due to factors beyond their control; or 3) that all citizens will be afforded equal opportunity to achieve what their potentials allow. Case Western Reserve University political scientist Robert Binstock rather succinctly describes the problem inherent in using equity between generations as a basis for policy-making:

> To describe the axis upon which equity is to be judged is to circumscribe the major options available for rendering justice. The contemporary preoccupation with so-called intergenerational equity blinds us to inequities within age groups and throughout our society.[24]

2. *"Numerical equality" is not an adequate definition of equity (fairness).* Implicit in the definition of fairness used by some who are concerned with perceived intergenerational inequities is the idea that per capita public expenditures on children and the elderly ought to be equal.

True, the elderly receive a larger per capita share of expenditures from all public sources—combined federal, state, and local—than do children. In separate analyses, Robert Clark and Joseph Spengler, and Mary Jo Bane estimate that the elderly receive about three times as much in direct public expenditures on a per capita basis as do children.[25] While it would be possible to refine this ratio by subtracting out both the proportion of social insurance benefits previously paid through payroll tax contributions and the current tax payments of the elderly, it seems reasonable to assume that the elderly would still receive a larger per capita share of public expenditures. Further, on average, the elderly have been less negatively affected by benefit reductions[26] and by the combined effect of benefit and tax reductions[27] during the first term of the Reagan administration than have other population groups.

It is tempting to accept such data as evidence that substantial intergenerational inequities exist. To draw such a conclusion, however, one must adopt an implicit definition of equity based on equal per capita public spending for children and the elderly.

While there is a certain intuitive appeal to equating equity (fairness) with numerical equality, they are not the same. Such a definition of equity is far too mechanical and narrow. It assumes that the relative needs of children and the elderly for public expenditures are identical and that equal expenditures are the equivalent of social justice. In fact, a sense of fairness based on the concept of need may require greater per capita expenditures for children than for the elderly, or substantial outlays for certain subgroups of children (e.g., the growing number of children living in poverty) but not for others. Even if the needs of each group were the same, equal per capita expenditures directed at each group in the face of substantial unmet needs do not result in equal outcomes, and thus do not add up to social justice.

Moreover, adopting this definition of equity might lead to another similarly narrow view of what constitutes fairness in the distribution of scarce resources among generations in a family. If equal per capita shares is accepted as the criterion for equity in distributing public resources to children and the elderly, it would seem reasonable to expect that the private intergenerational transfers that occur within the family (and that now go predominantly to children) ought to be equally distributed among the children and the elderly within a family unit. Of course, such a position would be preposterous.

3. *Social insurance programs serve different purposes from those of private insurance programs.* A very limited standard of fairness is sometimes used to evaluate Social Security (and Medicare, too). One frequently made argument is that certain groups of the young—especially higher-income workers—will not receive their money's worth out of these programs. Another is that today's young, as a group, will not have as high a rate of return on their ''investments'' in these programs as current retirees. Still another charges that since these programs do not function like private insurance programs, in which benefits are strictly related to the amount contributed, they are intergenerationally inequitable. For instance, a 30-year-old public health dentist writing in *Newsweek*'s ''My Turn'' column states:

> my husband and I paid $3,600 into the Social Security system in 1984. And that's just the amount deducted from our paychecks not the equal employer contribution that we also had to earn. If we'd been allowed to invest this $3,600 each year in an IRA earning 10 percent for 45 years, we could save more than 2.5 million dollars by retirement! Nausea prevents me from calculating the entire $7,200. How are older Americans faring today? Like bandits.[28]

145

Of course, if investments that could guarantee a 10 percent per year return (with inflation at 4 percent to 6 percent) for 45 years were readily available, perhaps everyone would be better off making such investments. Unfortunately, the real world does not work like that. Witness the depression of the 1930s or the high inflation and negative rates of return on investments of the late 1970s and early 1980s. In the real world, there is a need for social insurance programs that, by sharing risks, protect individuals and families—even those so fortunate that they earned enough in 1984 (at least $51,428) to be able to pay $3,600 in Social Security and Medicare payroll taxes.

As previously discussed in greater detail, the concept of fairness incorporated into these arguments is narrow and based on a misunderstanding of the multiple purposes of social insurance programs such as Social Security and Medicare (see chap. 4). These goals include preventing economic insecurity, enhancing the dignity of beneficiaries, and providing stable financing. Once it is understood that social insurance programs incorporate multiple goals, it becomes clear that compromise is necessary. For instance, to prevent economic insecurity, social insurance programs (such as Social Security and Medicare) must provide a floor of protection through special provisions for low-wage workers and certain family members, thereby emphasizing social adequacy.[29] Once this goal is incorporated, it becomes impossible to guarantee in addition that the rate of return for all parties will be identical. Further, as Haeworth Robertson, formerly chief actuary of the Social Security Administration, points out:

> Even to discuss this question of money's-worth (from the viewpoint of individuals) requires an underlying presumption that we have a national pension and social insurance program that provides—or should provide—benefits commensurate with an individual's contributions or a generation's contributions. This is, I believe, a false premise. We do not ask the question of individual money's worth about public education; we don't ask it about the national defense system; we don't ask it about the farm subsidy programs, or about Aid to Families with Dependent Children and a myriad of other welfare programs. And I am not sure that it is any more appropriate to ask the individual money's-worth question about social security than it is about any of these other national programs.[30]

If Social Security is being considered "intergenerationally inequitable"—in part because higher-income workers receive a lower rate of return—it would seem important to examine the fairness of tax expenditures for private pensions, IRAs, and the like, which also accrue disproportionately to such workers.

4. *The problems of the young do not result from excessive public expenditures on behalf of the elderly.* At times the intergenerational inequity framework seems based on a narrow interpretation of the principle that the young ought to have the same opportunity to share in the "American Dream" as their parents and grandparents had. From this point of view, the difficulties many young adults have in providing good employment, maintaining a comfortable standard of living, and buying a home in a period of relatively high interest rates are blamed on poor decisions of older age groups, especially the elderly. These decisions are viewed as causing federal deficits, large social expenditures directed at the elderly who are not in need, limited capital investment, and overinvestment in single-family homes.

These are the perceived intergenerational inequities that a new lobbying group—Americans for Generational Equity (AGE)—seeks to address by representing what it considers to be the interests of young Americans in shaping social policies that transfer resources between generations. A similar view of intergenerational inequity informs a *Washington Monthly* article by Phillip Longman entitled "Taking America to the Cleaners." In it, he argues that generational privileges of the old (defined as persons over 50) have turned the young (defined as persons under 30) into a new disadvantaged class in American society:

> Put bluntly, the old have come to insist that the young not only hold them harmless for their past profligacy, but sacrifice their own prosperity to pay for it. And, the beauty of it all, at least for the old, is that so far the young have not muttered a word of protest.[31]

AGE and others who hold this view are correct to be concerned about the very significant burden the large federal debt and high interest rates are placing on the young (and other age groups as well), just as they are about the high cost of home ownership and rental housing as well as about the relatively unfavorable economic conditions prevalent during most of the time baby boomers have been in the labor force. For example, a 17 December 1985 article in the *Wall Street Journal* points out:

The percentage of married couples in the 30- to 35-year-old age group who own homes has dropped to 70% from 75% since 1979. It is likely to keep dropping, says the National Association of Realtors, as more people in the group continue to rent.[32]

The article also notes:

The last two recessions took a toll on everybody's salary, but they hit those who were just entering the job market especially hard.... In real terms, the median income of men aged 25 to 34 fell 26% between 1973 and 1983, according to the Census Bureau. Average family income in this age group fell 14%.[33]

While younger cohorts face some significant problems, to assume these problems result chiefly from directing too many resources at the old seems too shortsighted. For example, it overlooks the role recent tax reductions combined with increases in defense spending have played in a growing federal debt. It overlooks the effect on the economy of changes in international markets. It overlooks the fact that many young adults have benefited from living in their parents' homes and that the equity accumulated in these homes will, for the most part, eventually be part of their inheritances.

Finally, it overlooks the many advantages younger cohorts enjoy thanks to the efforts of older ones. Today's young have benefited and will continue to benefit from the reduced incidence of childhood disease, increased life expectancies, generally larger inheritances left by parents, sacrifices made by the military during World War II, the opportunity for more education than their parents and grandparents had, etc. No doubt every cohort faces some hardships that might have been at least partly avoided by the actions of older birth cohorts. Every cohort, however, benefits from the actions of prior cohorts as well.

A VIRTUALLY UNMEASURABLE NOTION

It is virtually impossible to measure the concept of equity between generations as incorporated into the intergenerational inequity framework. Applying this concept to policy discussions generally involves measuring the flow of intergenerational transfers as part of an analysis designed to assess the fair distribution of public resources among generations. But apart from the difficulty of selecting the criterion to define fairness, numerous measurement problems undermine the utility of the intergenerational inequity framework as a basis for policy-making. We believe those who use this framework to assess social policy often fall into the trap of relying on very limited measures of the flow of resources between generations to justify their conclusion that substantial intergenerational inequities exist.

Intergenerational transfers are not simply government programs that transfer income and in-kind benefits between generations. Rather, they are both public and private responses to needs that occur throughout life. They also involve the legacies (e.g., economic growth, culture) older birth cohorts shape for those that follow and the heritage (e.g., inheritances, values) older generations within families transmit to younger and subsequent ones. When examined over time, intergenerational transfers are clearly seen to be two-way flows of resources from and to birth cohorts and individuals as they move through the life course.

The Scope of the Analysis Must Be Very Broad

Those who would accurately measure the various flows of resources between generations specifically to compare how different cohorts fare have set an impossible task for themselves. First, the scope of their analysis must be very broad. They must come to terms with the inability to draw conclusions about intergenerational inequity based on measurements of only one type of intergenerational transfer (e.g., Social Security). Since each generation receives transfers from those that precede it and gives transfers to those that follow, to reach accurate conclusions about intergenerational inequity requires an examination of transfers within the context of the multiple transfers occurring constantly between generations. But such an examination is really impossible since it requires answering questions such as the following:

• How should we value those economic and social investments made by previous generations that have resulted in intergenerational transfers?

• How should we value the economic and social investments made by current and future generations?

• How should we allocate the outcomes of investments made in research, conservation, environmental protection, and defense among generations?

• Should part of what is spent on the elderly be counted as a return on *their* investments in younger generations?

• Should part of what is spent on children be considered an investment in the future productivity of that society?

The Flow of Resources Over Time Must Be Measured

Second, those who would measure the flow of resources among generations—even if they do focus on only one type of intergenerational transfer—must apply the proper time perspective. As previously explained, a cross-sectional perspective identifies the flow of resources being transferred *at one point in time*. This approach tends to identify one age group—usually the old or the very young—as the receiver and another group—usually "working age" adults—as the giver. But the two-way flow of transfers over the life course makes it necessary to measure the flow of resources *over time* (that is, longitudinally) to get a more accurate picture of the benefits and costs of intergenerational transfers, and this approach is more complex than simply measuring the cross-sectional flow.

Indirect Benefits Must Be Counted

Third, those who would measure the flow of resources over time must come to terms with how they would value both the direct *and* indirect benefits of intergenerational transfers. Benefits of public and private transfers do not stop with the immediate recipient (see chaps. 1 and 4). To measure the relative costs and benefits of intergenerational transfers to different generations, some indirect and society-wide benefits need to be valued as they accrue to various generations.

Private Intergenerational Transfers Must Be Counted

Fourth, to measure the flow of resources among generations, it would be necessary to include, in addition to intergenerational transfers based on public policies, both societal and private intergenerational transfers, as well as their interactions in the calculus used to determine equity between generations. For example, since many transfers take place in the context of the family, just measuring how much younger cohorts contribute to the Social Security income of the elderly is not sufficient. It is also necessary to examine such factors as how the presence of Social Security affects inheritance flows from the elderly to the young.

Numerous Valuation Issues Remain

Measuring the flow of resources among generations to compare "who gets more" and "who gets less" gives rise to numerous valuation issues. A serious effort, for example, has to consider how to value current investments in research, environmental protection, and national defense. Since younger persons are likely to reap more benefit from such expenditures due to their longer life expectancies, it is reasonable to view many current budgetary expenditures as intergenerational transfers flowing largely from older to younger persons. An analyst should also assign values to increases in life expectancy and general improvements in the level of education that have occurred over time. Ultimately, attempts to measure equity between generations might lead to the illogical conclusion that very substantial intergenerational inequities do exist because the standard of living (no pun intended) for those who are currently alive is better, on average, than that experienced in the past.

In short, there is a major problem with trying to measure intergenerational transfers to compare the relative flows among generations: comprehensive measurement of these flows is virtually impossible and boggles the mind. As an alternative, analysts sometimes measure a particular resource transfer; for example, they identify trends in the percent of the federal budget directed at children versus the elderly. There is nothing necessarily wrong with making such limited measurements. The problem arises, however, when they are used as the basis for broad and inappropriate conclusions about equity between generations.

A "RED HERRING" APPROACH

Oddly enough, it turns out that the intergenerational inequity framework may actually *promote* intergenerational conflict and distract attention away from more useful ways of looking at social issues. It's a red herring. Although, as Binstock points out, "there is no systematic evidence of age group conflicts within the American populace as yet," the press, analysts, and policymakers increasingly frame issues in terms of intergenerational conflict.[34] In a Scripps-Howard wire service article entitled "Young, Old Clash Over Pace of Life in Sun Belt," which appeared in the *Pittsburgh Press* on 15 May 1984, Edward Cornish, editor of *Futurist Magazine*, is quoted as saying, "Up to now, young people didn't recognize their enemies, so to speak. They don't realize older people are elbowing them out of the government trough."[35] In the same vein, a headline on a front-page article in the 12 February

151

1985 *Washington Post* declares, "Florida's Generations Split Over Social Security."[36]

While there is always some tension between various groups in society, the bonds between generations are very strong, and there is little real evidence of significant intergenerational conflict. Successive birth cohorts and generations within families are interdependent, and many adhesives bind all generations together—including the multigenerational context of family life, the biological fact that all humans age, and the natural interdependence that circumstance and the varying needs across the life course impose.[37]

Certainly, examples can be found of substantial numbers of the elderly voting against a particular school-related tax or voting for politicians who favor laws prohibiting persons under age 50 from living in particular neighborhoods.[38] Such incidences, however, are only one small indicator of intergenerational relations, and one should not conclude from them that conflict between generations is the rule or that the elderly are a cohesive political group intent on forcing their will against the interests of the young (or vice versa). In fact, in spite of assertions by the press and senior advocacy organizations themselves about the existence of "senior power," "the voting behavior of the aging appears relatively stable and not susceptible to being changed substantially by age-based appeals."[39] Lifelong party affiliation, social class, race, and political beliefs exert greater influence than age on the voting behavior of the elderly. A recent review of the political participation of the elderly points out that "older persons are more notable for their similarities to other age groups than their differences."[40]

Further, while tensions might exist between successive birth cohorts and generations within families, there is little evidence that the elderly's political influence is resented, and public opinion polls consistently reveal a willingness to support programs for the elderly. For example, based on a representative sample of the population aged 18 and over, data from a 1981 Harris poll commissioned by the National Council on the Aging suggest that 64 percent of the adult population believed that, on the whole, the elderly had too little influence in 1981. Interestingly, younger persons were slightly more likely than the elderly to hold this opinion.[41] According to a poll commissioned by the American Council of Life Insurance, based on a representative sample of the noninstitutionalized population aged 18 and over in 1981, 67 percent favored increasing government spending on the elderly and only 4 percent favored reducing it.[42] A July 1985 Harris poll indicates that, given a choice between cutting defense spending or cutting programs that primarily benefit the elderly, the large majority of the public aged 18 and over would choose to cut defense spending. Specifically, 65 percent of persons aged 18 to 29, 73 percent of those aged 30 to 49, 73 percent of those aged 50 to 64, and 71 percent of the elderly voiced a preference for defense cuts rather than for "sharp cuts in Medicare benefits."[43]

Considerable evidence also exists to show that the elderly are concerned about meeting the needs of younger persons. For example, of the elderly who responded in a 1983 poll commissioned by the American Council of Life Insurance:

- 88 percent believed parents should feel a great deal or some responsibility to provide their grown children with a college education.

- 85 percent believed parents should feel a great deal or some responsibility to provide their grown children with a place to live if those children are unable to afford their own.

- 74 percent believed parents should feel a great deal or some responsibility to leave money to their grown children after they die.[44]

Distracts Attention from Important Issues

By framing issues in terms of conflict between generations, the intergenerational inequity framework distracts attention from more useful ways of looking at issues. Binstock points out that

> there is no inherent reason why issues of justice in allocating health care resources need to be framed on the basis of age. Better yet, one can frame trade-offs between expenditures in the arena of health care and other arenas.[45]

The lead article of a recent *Scientific American* exemplifies how the intergenerational inequity perspective can confound an important issue. In "Children and the Elderly in the U.S.," Samuel Preston, president of the Population Association of America, is primarily concerned about the seriousness of many problems facing children, but to make his point he uses the elderly as a comparison group.[46] He relies on trend data to argue that since "the early 1960's the well-being of the elderly has improved greatly whereas that of the young has deteriorated.''[47] During this same time, he points out, social expenditures for the elderly have increased, primarily—from his point of view—because of the political influence of the elderly, while many programs for children have been cut back.

Of course, many of the problems facing children that Preston identifies—very high poverty rates, family instability, the quality of public schools—urgently require attention. But they do so because it is important to respond to the needs of children—particularly those children who are at greatest risk—and *not* because the elderly or any other group for that matter are doing better or worse than children.

Preston has organized his argument in a manner that implies that whatever the elderly receive is at the expense of the young, and vice versa. But an approach to social policy that suggests we trade off the quality of life of one group for that of another is neither politically feasible nor desirable. Increasing the poverty rates of the elderly is hardly a satisfactory solution to the high rates of poverty among children.

The argument, as Preston and others have structured it, invites advocates of young and old to participate in divisive competition over resources. In this competition, the intergenerational inequity framework assumes a "fixed pie" of resources, which can only be cut from one of two places—either the elderly or the young. In doing so, it implicitly assumes that the governmental pie cannot be enlarged through economic growth or new tax revenues, and/or that expenditures for domestic programs cannot be increased by a reduction in defense spending. Consequently, it deflects attention from such important questions as 1) whether taxes should be raised to provide more resources for government programs to respond to dependency needs at all stages of the life course; 2) whether growing defense expenditures are crowding out social expenditures that are in the national interest; and 3) whether we ought to develop new policies to meet the needs of our most vulnerable citizens, regardless of age. In short, an approach to public policy that assumes that whatever is directed at one age group diminishes another invites policymakers and others to fall into the trap of encouraging intergenerational conflict rather than seek solutions to problems related to needs that exist across the life course.

CONCLUSION

Intergenerational inequity has become a catch-all slogan for a number of concerns, complaints, and calls for change in social policy. It also imposes a way of looking at policy issues—that is, a framework—

that presents the issues in terms of competition between young and old over the division of scarce resources and that generally assumes that policy for the elderly as currently structured is "unfair" to younger persons. While many concerns raised under the rubric of intergenerational inequity (e.g., poverty among children, budget deficits) are important public policy issues, we believe that framing them in terms of competition between generations could contribute to a variety of negative or unintended policy outcomes.

First, intergenerational inequity—as both a framework and a slogan—fosters numerous misconceptions about the intergenerational benefits flowing from policies for the elderly. These misconceptions could undermine public support for critical income, health, and social service programs that benefit persons of all ages. Should these programs, in turn, be reduced or eliminated, today's middle-aged and young people could suffer both because these protections would not be available when they reach old age and because they would not receive many of the indirect benefits they now receive.

Second, the intergenerational inequity framework and slogan encourages divisive competition between advocates for policies directed primarily at particular age groups. Ultimately, such competition will serve only the interests of those wishing to reduce the government's role in providing social welfare in response to needs across the life course. Orville Brim, Jr., formerly of the Foundation for Child Development, warns:

> If I were working at DoD [Department of Defense] I would be laughing as I saw those concerned separately with old and young people fighting over their pitiful allotment, splitting their forces, taking from each other, engaged in a war of old versus young, and unable to organize into a common cause.[48]

Third, as a way of approaching public policies, this framework could undermine the willingness of all parties to participate in intergenerational transfers critical to social stability and progress. Social progress requires not only individual effort and achievement but also cooperation between generations in society and in families, particularly in meeting the various needs that occur throughout life. By emphasizing conflict and by potentially undermining support for intergenerational transfers based on public policies, the intergenerational inequity framework runs counter to the notion of social progress.

Fourth, the framework could distract attention from more useful ways of evaluating and making social policy.

Fifth, policies emanating from such a framework could undermine the care-giving functions of the family. If, for example, intergenerational inequity were used as the reason for government not to respond to the growing pressures on families for care-giving, many families could be overwhelmed by the stresses (financial, emotional) inherent in providing extra-ordinary care to their family members.

There is one more very important reason to be wary of the intergenerational inequity framework as a basis for policy-making. While those who use this approach come from across the political spectrum, we believe that, at least for some proponents, this framework may be simply a convenient rationale for a political ideology that opposes virtually all public efforts directed at meeting family and individual needs. While acknowledging the sincerity of these advocates, we believe this rationale ignores the private/public approach to problem solving and the rich mix of values inherent in our pluralistic society. The intergenerational inequity viewpoint may be a smoke screen for some ideas that are at odds with traditional values and commitments of our society.

At best, then, the framing of issues in terms of conflict between generations is based on a misunderstanding of relations between generations and distracts attention from more appropriate ways of examining social issues. At worst, it is a cynical and divisive strategy put forth to justify and build political support for a view that rejects the traditional public involvement in meeting needs across the life course.

Just as people of *all* ages have a stake in policies serving the needs of the elderly, so do *all* ages have a stake in how our society responds to such challenges as meeting the needs of children and families and combating a growing federal deficit. However, we will not find satisfactory answers to these and other critical challenges through an approach that pits generation against generation in competition for resources. Wisdom in this instance begins with recognizing that to have needs is a universal rather than an isolated condition, and with understanding that each individual and each generation has a common stake in society's response to these needs.

Notes

1. Note that our view of intergenerational inequity has benefited from discussions with members of the Steering Committee of The Gerontological Society of America as well as with Robert H. Binstock, Msgr. Charles Fahey, and Bernice Neugarten, and from an article by Robert H. Binstock, "The Oldest Old: A Fresh Perspective on Compassionate Ageism Revisited," *Milbank Memorial Fund Quarterly/ Health and Society* 63, no. 2 (n.d.).

2. Richard D. Lamm, *Mega-Traumas, America at the Year 2000* (Boston, Mass.: Houghton Mifflin, 1985), 52-53.

3. Manuel Schiffres, "Next: Young vs. Old?" The Editor's Page, *U.S. News & World Report*, 5 November 1984, 94.

4. Internal Revenue Service, *Individual Income Tax Returns: 1982 Statistics of Income*, publication 79 (10-84) (Washington, D.C.: U.S. Department of the Treasury, 1984), 73.

5. Alvin Schorr, *". . . Thy Father and Thy Mother . . . ,"* 24.

6. Robert H. Binstock, "The Aged as Scapegoat," *The Gerontologist* 23 (April 1983): 136.

7. Joseph F. Quinn, "The Economic Status of the Elderly: Beware of the Mean," *The Review of Income and Wealth* (1986, forthcoming).

8. Jerry Flint, "The Old Folks," *Forbes*, 18 February 1980, 51.

9. Council of Economic Advisors, *Economic Report of the President* [and] *Annual Report of the Council of Economic Advisors* (Washington, D.C.: U.S. GPO, 1985), 160.

10. See, for example, Michael Hurd and John B. Shoven, "Real Income and Wealth of the Elderly," *AEA Papers and Proceedings* 72, no. 2 (n.d.); Marilyn Moon and Isabel V. Sawhill, "Family Incomes: Gainers and Losers," in *The Reagan Record*, ed. John L. Palmer and Isabel V. Sawhill (Cambridge, Mass.: Ballinger Publishing Co., 1984).

11. Marilyn Moon, "The Impacts of Poverty on Elderly Women and Minorities" (Paper prepared for the Thirty-seventh Annual Scientific Meeting of The Gerontological Society of America, San Antonio, Tex., 18 November 1984).

12. Bureau of the Census, "Money Income and Poverty Status: 1984," 11.

13. Bureau of the Census, "Money Income and Poverty Status: 1984."

14. Timothy M. Smeeding, "Nonmoney Income and the Elderly: The Case of the 'Tweeners' " (Paper prepared for the Sixth Annual APPAM Research Conference, New Orleans, La., 18-20 October 1984, Mimeographed).

15. Bureau of the Census, "Projections of the Population: 1983-2080," 7-8.

16. Ibid.

17. Schiffres, "Next: Young vs. Old?" 84.

18. Phillip Longman, "Justice Between Generations," *Atlantic Monthly*, June 1985, 73.

19. Barbara Boyle Torrey, "Guns vs. Canes: The Fiscal Implications of an Aging Population," *AEA Papers and Proceedings* 72, no. 2 (n.d.); Joseph A. Califano,

"The Aging of America: Questions for the Four Generation Society," *Annals of the American Academy of Political and Social Science* 438 (n.d.); June O'Neill, unpublished material prepared for the CBO, 1978 (estimates summarized in James Storey and Gary Hendricks, "Retirement Income Issues in an Aging Society," unpublished paper, Urban Institute, December 1979); Barbara Boyle Torrey, "Technical Details on the Projection of Federal Outlays for the Older Population" (Washington, D.C.: Office of Management and Budget, 1981); Robert L. Clark and John A. Menefee, "Federal Expenditures for the Elderly: Past and Future," *The Gerontologist* 21 (April 1981): 18; Bureau of the Census, "Projections of the Population: 1983-2080," 6.

20. These dependency ratios are based on middle series projections in Bureau of the Census, "Projections of the Population: 1983-2080," table D.

21. Torrey, "Technical Details."

22. William H. Crown, "Some Thoughts on Reformulating the Dependency Ratio," *The Gerontologist* 25 (April 1985): 166-171.

23. William H. Crown, "The Prospective Burden of an Aging Population" (Mimeographed).

24. Binstock, "The Oldest Old," 437-438.

25. Robert L. Clark and Joseph J. Spengler, "Dependency Ratios: Their Use in Economic Analyses," *Research in Population Economics* 2 (1980); Mary Jo Bane, "Trends in Public Spending on Children and Their Families," in *American Families and Their Economy*, ed. Richard R. Nelson and Felicity Skidmore (Washington, D.C.: National Academy of Sciences, 1983).

26. Patricia Ruggles and Marilyn Moon, "The Impact of Recent Legislative Changes in Benefit Programs for the Elderly," *The Gerontologist* 25 (April 1985): 153.

27. Moon and Sawhill, "Family Incomes: Gainers and Losers."

28. Teresa A. Anderson, "The Best Years of Their Lives," My Turn, *Newsweek*, 7 January 1985.

29. Ball, *Social Security Today and Tomorrow*, 1-17.

30. Haeworth Robertson, paper in response to Robert J. Myers and Bruce D. Schobel, "A Money's-Worth Analysis of Social Security Retirement Benefits," *Transactions, Society of Actuaries* (1983), 552-553.

31. Phillip Longman, "Taking America to the Cleaners," *Washington Monthly*, November 1982, 24.

32. Betsy Morris, "Strapped Yuppies, Many Baby Boomers Find They Are Caught in a Financial Squeeze," *Wall Street Journal*, 17 December 1985.

33. Ibid.

34. Binstock, "The Oldest Old," 432.

35. Stephen Wissink, "Young, Old Clash over Pace of Life in Sun Belt," *Pittsburgh Press*, 15 May 1984.

36. Juan Williams, "Florida's Generations Split over Social Security," *Washington Post*, 12 February 1985, 1.

37. Bernice L. Neugarten, comments in invited symposium, "Intergenerational Con-

flict: Fact or Fiction?'' (Thirteenth International Congress of Gerontology, New York, 16 July 1985).

38. See, for example, Wissink, "Young, Old Clash."

39. Robert B. Hudson and Robert H. Binstock, "Political Systems and Aging," in *Handbook of Aging and the Social Sciences*, ed. Robert H. Binstock and Ethel Shanas, 1st ed. (New York: Van Nostrand Reinhold Co., 1976), 388.

40. Robert B. Hudson and John Strate, "Aging and Political Systems," in *Handbook of Aging and the Social Sciences*, ed. Binstock and Shanas, 2d ed., 566.

41. Louis Harris and Associates, Inc., *Aging in the Eighties: America in Transition* (Washington, D.C.: National Council on the Aging, Inc., 1981).

42. Data provided by the American Council of Life Insurance.

43. Louis Harris and Associates, Inc., poll, 1 July 1985, table 52 (unpublished data).

44. Data provided by the American Council of Life Insurance.

45. Binstock, "The Oldest Old," 433.

46. Preston, "Children and the Elderly in the U.S.," 49.

47. Ibid., 44.

48. Orville G. Brim, Jr., "Some Policy Implications of Life Span Development Research" (New York: Foundation for Child Development, n.d., Mimeographed).

9

Generational Interdependence: A Real-World Base for Policy

THIS REPORT focuses on what joins rather than divides the interests of all generations. In it we show why, in an interdependent and aging society, all generations have a common stake in intergenerational transfers that assist individuals and families in responding to needs existing at all points across the life course—ranging from the care given in families, to publicly funded transfers such as Social Security and education, to economic growth.

In stressing the importance of thinking about society and the life course as a whole, the report illustrates how policies directed at one age group generally affect all others, at any point in time and over time, as the members of particular age groups grow older. It points out that intergenerational transfers are not simply government programs but include a variety of private exchanges within the family and the private sector as well as broad societal transfers. And it suggests that in developing public policy, it is a mistake to focus on the interests of any particular age group or birth cohort without also recognizing the impacts such policies will have across all age groups and birth cohorts and on family members of all ages.

We also stress the importance of all levels of government sharing the burden with individuals and families of meeting the needs of persons of all ages. In a complex and interdependent society like ours, indi-

160

vidual autonomy and independence remain, as they should, cherished values; to maximize these values, we must seek an appropriate balance between individual, family, and governmental efforts.

In chapter 1, we noted that our decision to write this report was prompted by the tone and character of a debate being generated by an approach to public policy—the intergenerational inequity approach—that frames issues in terms of competition and conflict between generations. Although we recognize there are well-informed and well-motivated persons who have reached different conclusions, we believe this approach is based on 1) misunderstandings about what the demographics of our aging society imply; 2) limited understandings about the interdependence of all generations in society and the common stake in intergenerational transfers; 3) failure to recognize the diversity that exists within all age groups; 4) narrow definitions of equity between generations; and 5) limited measures of the flow of selected resources between generations, which are then used as a basis for reaching broad conclusions about the fairness of public policy (see chap. 8). And our concern is that the point of view behind this approach leads to particular policy prescriptions that could, if widely accepted, determine how the nation responds to the challenge of an aging society.

CONCLUSIONS ABOUT THE INTERGENERATIONAL INEQUITY FRAMEWORK

The intergenerational inequity approach to public policy incorporates a deep pessimism about the implications of an aging society. It presents the twentieth-century trend of increasing longevity and the significant improvements of the past 30 years in the economic well-being of most elderly persons as if these changes somehow reflect the failure of our society rather than some of its greatest achievements. It is pessimistic about the ability of the economy of the future to meet the needs of all citizens, and it implies that we are relatively powerless to confront some of the problems emerging in an aging society despite, for example, newly developed technology and research-based knowledge. Perhaps, most importantly, in painting the aging society almost entirely in negative tones, it fails to recognize opportunities associated with this demographic event, including increased quality of life for today's young when they are old, and the opportunity—and necessity—to use the productive abilities of future cohorts of the elderly as fully as possible.

Finally, it is pessimistic in its conviction that perceived intergenerational inequities are promoting substantial intergenerational conflict.

Although there is always some tension between various groups in society, the bonds between generations are very strong and there is little real evidence of significant intergenerational conflict. Thus, our examination of the intergenerational inequity approach to public policy has led us to the following conclusions:

- It distracts attention away from more important ways of framing policy issues related to the challenge of an aging society.

- At best, it is based on a misunderstanding of the relationships between generations and on a narrow interpretation of equity between generations.

- At worst, it is little more than a cynical and purposely divisive rationale put forth to justify reductions in programs that benefit all age groups.

OBSERVATIONS BASED ON THE COMMON STAKE

Our approach to understanding the challenges of an aging society grows out of a recognition of the common stake all generations have in intergenerational transfers. Much of this report illustrates this common stake and discusses how this point of view promotes a broader understanding of the implications of policies directed at any one age group. This discussion leads to the following observations:

- Over the course of their lives, individuals generally both give and receive care within their families. Because the family is generally the preferred source of care, all generations have a stake in social policies that support and enhance its ability to provide this care.

- Social Security provides an excellent example of an inter-generational transfer based on public policy for which the benefits and costs are widely distributed across all generations. It is erroneous to view this transfer as a one-way flow from young to old. The common stake in Social Security also grows out of both the preference of individuals and families for a dignified and stable means of support for the elderly, the disabled, and surviving and financially dependent family members as well as the centrality of Social Security to the economic welfare of beneficiaries, now and for the foreseeable future.

162

• Because intergenerational transfers such as public education and Social Security are critical to the functioning of society and because demographic and economic change is an ongoing process, such policies must be carefully reviewed and policy options vigorously debated. However, to understand fully the consequences of various policy options, it is critical that those considering changes understand the common stake in these intergenerational transfers. Unfortunately, this aspect of transfers is frequently ignored.

• Societal intergenerational transfers such as economic growth, knowledge, and culture are fundamental to each generation's progress and continuity. Investments made in promoting such transfers are generally more beneficial to younger and subsequent generations and are necessary responses to the various challenges of the future. For example, investments in research on aging are an intergenerational transfer that may improve the quality of life for future cohorts of the elderly and also help society respond to the challenge of an aging population.

• The elderly, now and in the future, have at least two important stakes in programs that respond to the needs of children, young adults, and the middle-aged. First, they benefit directly and indirectly from education, training, and health programs that help increase the productivity of the work force. Second, it is in their political self-interest to avoid a politics that pits generations against each other.

• Younger generations have two important stakes in programs that assist the elderly in maintaining a decent quality of life. First, they will be served by those programs when they become old. Second, programs that enable their grandparents and parents to remain as autonomous as possible in old age relieve younger families of financial burdens and intrafamily stresses.

• Advocates for the elderly should be as concerned about the quality of life for future elderly generations as they are about that for the current elderly. Since quality of life in old age is largely related to circumstances throughout a person's life, advocates for the elderly have a special responsibility to actively support policies designed to improve the opportunities for and the income and health status of people of all ages, not just the elderly.

163

• In particular, for both humanitarian and practical reasons, advocates for the elderly and others concerned with preparing for the retirement of the baby boomers have a special responsibility to support educational, health, employment, and income policies that respond to the needs and aspirations of the many poor and near-poor children in America. As the baby boomers reach retirement ages, today's poor children will be reaching prime working ages. Failure to provide them with adequate educational and employment opportunities now could undermine their future productivity and reduce the quality of life for the baby boomers in retirement.

THE COMMON STAKE AND THE AGING OF SOCIETY

The framework we propose—the common stake—we believe is in keeping with traditional American values and will be of use in preparing for an aging society. It suggests that we need not shrink from the challenge of an aging society and that this challenge can be met without trading off the needs of one age group for those of another. As a society, we can prepare for the aging of America in several ways—for example, by making public and private decisions that stimulate economic growth; by investing in research that can potentially improve the quality of life for future cohorts of the elderly while also reducing the anticipated rate of increase in health care costs; by providing the option for persons of all ages to contribute to the economy and their communities for as long as they are willing and able; and by supporting an approach to public policy that recognizes the great desire and potential of the elderly, now and in the future, to make ongoing contributions to all aspects of society.

By concentrating on what joins rather than divides the interests of generations, we do not intend to suggest that these interests are identical or that they never conflict. Certainly there are times when one generation is forced to bear particularly heavy burdens (e.g., the generation that fought World War II), and there are times when difficult decisions (which can affect age groups differently) must be made over allocation of funds, be they federal, state, local, or even family funds. Rather, we focus on the common stake because we believe the interdependence of all generations is at the root of the continuity and progress of society. An approach to public policy that does not build on this understanding—or, even worse, that threatens to strain the bonds between generations—does not present a realistic framework from which to prepare for the future.

Policy recommendation. Most policy reports on the aging of America end with a listing of recommendations for specific changes in health, income, and social service policies. This has never been our intent.

Instead, we chose first to identify how the framework that is applied to policy debates concerning the challenge of our aging society can affect 1) the perception of problems and opportunities associated with the aging of America, 2) the policy options considered, and 3) the future direction of policy; and second to present a framework—based on an understanding of the common stake in intergenerational transfers—that we believe will be of use in these policy discussions. Our single recommendation is not that this framework should necessarily be adopted. We recommend, rather, that *those concerned with responding to the challenge of an aging society understand the power of various frameworks to define the terms of debate, and therefore give careful consideration to the various ways this debate can be framed and to the implications these approaches to policy-making can have for persons of all ages.*

In conclusion, a sufficiently broad policy framework for responding to the challenge of an aging society must include a concern for the long-term welfare of all age groups, an appreciation of policies that support the family as an institution, and an understanding of the significance of public and private investments in the human resources that will define the possibilities of the future.

Afterword:
A Research Agenda*

W RITING this report has provided us with an opportunity to think about intergenerational relations in an aging society. The research agenda that follows identifies five broad topics—each related to some intergenerational themes discussed in the report—that need to be addressed to prepare for an aging society.

By suggesting research topics (and specific research issues and questions that illustrate their importance), we do not mean to present the definitive research agenda on aging. Obviously, numerous research topics (and related issues and questions) could be identified as part of such an agenda. What we do instead is highlight several topics that grow out of this report and that require more information if we are to better understand intergenerational relations and the life course in an aging society. These topics are

- research that enhances our knowledge of the interdependence of generations and the exchanges that occur across the life course;

- research on how events and interventions throughout life affect old age;

- research on the value issues involved in allocating and distributing resources in an aging society;

*As part of its new Program on Emerging Issues in Aging, The Gerontological Society received funding from the National Institute on Aging (NIA) to develop a research agenda related to the issues discussed in this report. This afterword and most of chapter 5 are drawn from a report submitted to NIA under separate cover.

• research on ethical issues confronting an aging society; and

• research on what attitudes all generations have toward old age and on how these attitudes affect behavior.

The following points should be noted. First, most research topics are selected to suggest both a perspective (e.g., a life course approach) and a potentially fruitful area of investigation. Second, since the agenda reflects the multidisciplinary and crosscutting nature of research on aging, each topic suggests research issues or questions suitable for both investigation in various disciplines (e.g., biology, economics, philosophy) and investigation concerned with various issues (e.g., housing, economic welfare, health). Finally, the specific research issues and questions identified under each broad topic below simply exemplify the *type* of research that needs to be conducted in each area; many other issues and questions could also be incorporated under each topic. We hope others will wish to add to this agenda.

Research That Furthers Understanding of the Interdependence of Generations and Exchanges

Intergenerational transfers based on public policy (e.g., Medicare, Aid to Families with Dependent Children), those that are private (e.g., care-giving, inheritances), and those that are societal (e.g., economic growth) are essential for both meeting human needs and contributing to the continuity and progress of society. While at one point in time, particular individuals and cohorts may be more on the giving or receiving end of these exchanges, over the life course individuals and cohorts both contribute to and benefit from these exchanges.

In preparing for an aging society, it is important to better understand the multiple flows of resources between generations and how they contribute to the continuity and progress of society. Research is needed that 1) examines the bonds between generations; 2) assesses how changes in public policies might affect the flow of public and private resources between generations; and 3) assesses the impact of such changes on the family life and well-being of particular groups.

For example, since job turnover in the labor force is partially related to retirement policy, it is important to assess the sensitivity of this exchange to changes in public policies such as the tax policies governing private pensions. Similarly, since care-giving to family members represents an intergenerational transfer of great value to an aging society, policymakers need to better understand the flow of private resources in the care-giving process as well as how changes in public policy may encourage or discourage a family's care-giving functions.

In analyzing the flow of resources between generations, two methodological issues are of special importance. First, a "systems perspective" is needed, which identifies the multiple impacts of intergenerational transfers. For instance, what impact do government transfers have, not just on particular groups (e.g., disabled workers, the elderly) identified as beneficiaries, but also on other groups (e.g., family members, young taxpayers) and on the society as a whole? In short, both direct and indirect transfers need to be more clearly identified.

Second, the time perspective incorporated into an analysis may partially shape the policy implications drawn from research. We have noted, for example, how a cross-sectional view of the flow of resources in Social Security and Medicare suggests that it is mainly the elderly who benefit and younger persons who pay for these programs, whereas a longitudinal view suggests that the costs and benefits of these programs are shared over time.

Below are examples of the types of research questions (along with brief background statements) that need to be addressed for a better understanding of interdependence and intergenerational exchanges:

1) Housing policy and program-planning decisions are, or should be, based on considerations regarding intergenerational relationships. In one sense, housing over the life course can be viewed as a succession of shared residential arrangements in which one begins as a dependent child living with one's parents and may end up in old age either relying on one's children for assistance or, in some cases, actually living with them. Many housing-related policies influence whether housing and neighborhoods support persons of all ages or only specific age cohorts. These policies include building codes that affect the layout of dwelling units; the location of housing in relation to facilities and services (e.g., schools, shopping centers, transportation, and senior citizens centers); and zoning that either encourages or discourages multiunits as well as single-family units.[1] In preparing for an aging society, then, research is needed to address the following issues:

• What impact do housing-related subsidies have on the entire family as opposed to only the targeted person?

• To what extent do social investments (e.g., funds for Social Security, Medicare, home-based care, and childrens' services) broaden family members' residential options?[2]

• Which policies facilitate individual choice in whether generations maintain residences that are physically proximate?[3]

• Which policies (e.g., reverse annuity mortgages, home repair programs, home care services) give older people the option of remaining in their homes as they age and/or experience problems related to income or physical limitations? Which policies (e.g., congregate housing) encourage older people to move to more supportive environments?[4]

• To what extent are the assets of one generation passed on to succeeding generations through housing stock? How do policies concerning reverse annuity mortgages, capital gains taxes, and property tax abatements affect the asset flows between generations and the decisions of older people to retain their own homes?[5]

• Which policies encourage intergenerational neighborhoods, housing developments, and mixed age housing (which provides for separate as well as shared living spaces and facilities) through facility planning for all ages?

2) Under the most commonly accepted intermediate assumptions—the combined Old-Age and Survivors Insurance and Disability Insurance trust funds—Social Security is scheduled to build up very substantial surpluses beginning in the 1990s and continuing to about 2020. After that, the reserves are scheduled to be drawn down to pay for the retirement of the baby boomers and those who follow.[6] The following issues need to be examined:

• What are the potential macroeconomic effects (e.g., on savings) of this projected surplus?

• What are the implications of such a surplus on the federal deficit?

• What are the implications of such a surplus on investment options?

• What are the intergenerational implications of the projected surplus?

• What are the merits of alternative policy options (e.g., reducing payroll taxes earmarked for OASDI and moving to a floating tax rate)?

169

3) In an interdependent society, investments made or not made by one generation usually have a variety of impacts on other generations. Research is needed on how investments made in the education of children affect their future productivity and, in turn, affect the retirement circumstances of their elders. More specifically,

- What does existing public education of low-income children imply for current and future retirees and especially baby boomers?

- How sensitive is future productivity (and ability to support a retired population) to various levels of investment in public education?

4) What kind of impact does (and will) the increased number and proportion of women in the work force have on the different kinds of care-giving exchanges that occur within the family?[7]

5) What impact would greater availability of governmental home care services or private long-term care insurance that allows one to purchase such services have on the amount and kind of family care-giving to older relatives requiring long-term care?[8]

Research on How Events and Interventions Throughout Life Affect Old Age

Quality of life in old age is partially determined by experiences throughout the life course, including the lifelong effects of social structure, the impact of social policies, the particular set of historical circumstances that affect each cohort, personal decisions, and chance.* Research is needed that examines how circumstances throughout life (e.g., access to health care, preventive health care, race and sex discrimination, access to education) have affected the well-being of current cohorts of the elderly and are likely to affect that of future ones. In particular, to what extent do interventions and events at one stage of life (e.g., "Head Start," early and periodic screening for health problems, exposure to health risks) have implications for later stages (including old age). For instance, just as research has shown that supplemental doses of calcium prior to menopause can reduce the risk of osteoporosis (see chap. 6), biomedical research on events early in life could result in breakthroughs and interventions that would delay the onset of or possibly even eliminate certain debilitating conditions. The

---

*It is important to remember that a life course perspective also suggests that individuals retain the capacity to change throughout life.

information produced by such studies will be valuable in developing policies designed to improve the quality of life for future cohorts of the elderly and can conceivably change the anticipated cost of meeting their health care needs.

1) Additional research is prompted by

• the need to know more about the critical periods during the life course when the effects of specific health and social risk factors are likely to be of greater concern for the elderly;[9]

• the need to understand more about the risk factors that indicate subsequent need for long-term care;[10]

• the need to better understand interactions among risk factors as they affect the timing of disease, rate of disease progression, and age at death;[11]

• the need to make better predictions about the health of the next elderly cohort by using longitudinal studies that assess the health of individuals as they age and by examining differences across cohorts;[12] and

• the need to know more about early indications of decline in the function of older people to anticipate the problems they will face and to make better decisions about future actions (e.g., estate planning, retirement, treatment alternatives).[13]

2) Basic biomedical research has shown that manipulation of the environment and nutrition early in life can have profound effects on an individual's old age. This has been amply illustrated in biological experiments on rodents. For instance, progressive deterioration of the kidneys in rodents results in death due to kidney failure for 50 percent of rats in old age. However, if their food intake is restricted beginning in young adulthood, progression of this disease is so retarded that less than 5 percent of rats die of kidney failure.[14] While it is impossible to perform a comparable longitudinal study of humans, "there is certainly reason to believe that, as is the case for rodents, manipulations early in the life of a person can markedly influence the biological characteristics of that person in old age."[15] Therefore, biomedical research is needed to examine how various environmental and nutritional interventions introduced early in the life of an organism can affect outcomes later in its life course.

Research on the Value Issues Involved in Allocating and Distributing Resources in an Aging Society

Concern with the fairness of allocating and distributing resources in an aging society partially motivated the writing of this report. As suggested earlier, the framework used to clarify policy choices and to define fairness as well as the allocative and distributive decisions that follow express particular values or a particular constellation of values. As some researchers have stated,

> no matter how seemingly objective we attempt to construct the process of choice in formulating national policy—on aging or anything else for that matter—we must confront value questions in some orderly, critical, and reasonable way.[16]

Significant allocative and distributive decisions are being and will be made in response to the growing elderly population. Failure to identify values involved in these choices does not mean that the policy outcomes will not involve trade-offs between values; it means only that such trade-offs will not be obvious and that decisions will sometimes be made without recognition of what is being lost. Thus, research is needed that identifies and clarifies the values behind various approaches to allocating and distributing resources in an aging society. Below are examples of the types of questions and issues requiring further research:

• What values inform the models of intergenerational obligations to which we adhere in our society? What do these models imply for the exchange of resources between generations in the family and in society?[17]

• What values inform public policies determining who shall be eligible for organ transplantation or dialysis procedures, as well as for government subsidy of such procedures?[18]

• In our society, most care-giving to frail individuals is provided by families and friends. What values inform the extent to which and circumstances under which such care-giving is considered the responsibility of the family versus that of the public?[19]

• What values inform different approaches to allocating health care resources across the life course? For example, what are the value implications of using age-based versus functional criteria as the basis for rationing certain procedures?

Research on Ethical Issues Confronting an Aging Society

While not addressed directly in this report, the ethical issues confronting an aging society have very significant implications for relations between generations. For instance, the interaction of an aging society with social policies and advances in biomedical technology can result in numerous ethical dilemmas for individuals and for family members of all ages, as well as for service providers and society at large.

Some of the most familiar ethical concerns before individuals, family members, and professionals who deliver services are related to the ability of medical technology to keep people alive, in many cases long after their quality of life has radically diminished. With more people living to advanced old age, dilemmas relating to the ethics of providing or withholding costly life-extending treatments will be more common.

Social policies, too, impose ethical dilemmas on individuals, family members, and society as a whole. For example, the "spend-down" provision in Medicaid, which requires a household to reduce resources to a very low level before a physically disabled or ill spouse is eligible for Medicaid, often forces healthy spouses to choose between their own economic welfare and the health care needs of their partner. Similarly, the presence or absence of laws governing the legitimacy of "living wills" and statutory provisions concerning guardianship of persons or property also condition the types of ethical issues before individuals, families, and the society.

Thus, research is needed that both identifies and discusses alternative resolutions—including their implications for all age groups—of the ethical issues and questions that naturally grow out of an aging society. Below are examples of such issues and questions requiring additional research:

- Our social policies treat every frail population differently (e.g., older Americans with severe rheumatoid arthritis, children with multiple sclerosis, middle-aged paraplegics). What are the ethical implications of this differential treatment?[20]

- What are the ethical implications of "targeting" resources to certain subgroups of the population and of withholding resources from others? In particular, how should family resources be considered in this context—*instead of* or *as supplemental to* public-sector services? Do we concentrate public resources on those whose family support is meager, or do we try to supplement and shore up family support with public resources?[21]

173

• What constitutes ethical behavior regarding the use of scientific discoveries that might slow the biological aging process? As a society, we need to debate publicly whether application of such processes necessarily benefits the individual and/or society.[22]

• What ethical underpinning correctly informs societal standards for determining when individuals are no longer mentally and/or physically competent to take care of themselves or manage their own affairs?[23]

Research on What Attitudes All Generations Have Toward Old Age and How These Attitudes Affect Behavior

Attitudes and expectations about the elderly and about one's own aging can affect 1) the types of policies and programs particular cohorts and/or socioeconomic groups are willing to support (in particular, policies that respond to the needs of the elderly); 2) the willingness of individuals to participate in private exchanges; and 3) the behavior of individuals and cohorts as they age. In a society in which continuity and progress require cooperation between all generations, it is important to understand attitudes about aging and the elderly that exist among various groups. For example, how does the image of old age among current workers relate to their willingness to pay Social Security taxes? How do the image and expectations of old age among elderly cohorts and groups affect their willingness to pay taxes in support of services to other age groups? Finally, how do different groups (e.g., younger minority workers) view the elderly and those programs that transfer resources to them?

Research is also needed on how expectations are formed among cohorts of what old age is like and on how these expectations affect behavior (e.g., savings, planned retirement age, exercise, and health maintenance). Such information is necessary for individuals to plan for old age.

Below are examples of the types of research issues and questions that need to be addressed on attitudes toward old age:

• Because minorities in this country have a different, somewhat younger age distribution than the nonminority population, they may tend to view the distribution of resources and delivery of services to various age groups somewhat differently than nonminorities.[24] How does variation in attitudes among racial and ethnic groups regarding resource transfers affect preferences for and delivery of services to various age groups?

- We need to understand more about what different constituencies (e.g., consumers, providers, payers, families) prefer concerning the provision of care. What outcomes of care are preferred in different circumstances? For instance, when is preserving life *not* the prime goal?[25]

- We need to determine how much care older people want. How much are they willing to pay for it?[26]

- How does cohort-related variation in attitudes toward old age and toward people who are currently elderly explain or predict behaviors such as labor force participation in old age, a life-style conducive to good health in old age, or choice of health maintenance options and savings alternatives for the retirement years?[27]

- How do cohort or historical effects influence the intergenerational transmission of values? For instance, has the experience of being raised during the depression of the 1930s, when people had many familial responsibilities, led to values for those now in their sixties that stress self-sufficiency in the care-giving to frail parents?[28]

CONCLUSION

This research agenda presents five broad research topics (and related research questions and issues) that are tied to the intergenerational themes explored in the report. It is not intended as an exhaustive listing of research issues that need to be addressed to prepare for an aging society. In fact, this agenda, in its organization and presentation, does not easily lend itself to identifying many types of research issues, including some that may have significant—even revolutionary—implications for all generations.

In particular, certain types of basic biomedical research directed at nonaging-related topics could have unexpected spin-offs and might, for example, alter the quality of life for all age groups. For example, basic research in molecular genetics is leading to new knowledge of how the so-called slow viruses work (e.g., *herpus* viruses), of how the autoimmune system in AIDS and other diseases involving the autoimmune system function, and of how organs such as the heart and liver change in their ability to function over the life course.[29] It is no less true that basic research directed at improving the quality of life for everyone can lead to improvements in the quality of life for older people in particular. Analyzing the structural and functional components of the heart, for instance, also leads to a better understanding of the processes—often manifested only in old age—involved in heart deterioration and disease.

Research into the topics we have identified may have important implications for intergenerational relations in an aging society. So, too, investments in basic biomedical, behavioral, and social science research addressed to a variety of concerns other than those already identified here may have unpredicted benefits that affect all aspects of an aging society—including intergenerational relations.

Notes

1. Material adapted from a symposium developed by M. Powell Lawton, director, Behavioral Research, Philadelphia Geriatric Center.

2. Ibid.

3. Ibid.

4. Jon Pynoos, director, Program Policy and Services Research, Andrus Gerontology Center, University of Southern California, personal communication, 24 December 1985.

5. Ibid.

6. Alicia Munnell and Lynn E. Blais, "Do We Want Large Social Security Surpluses," *New England Economic Review* (September/October 1984): 5.

7. Marjorie H. Cantor, Brookdale Professor of Gerontology, Fordham University, personal communication, 23 November 1985.

8. Ibid.

9. Gordon H. DeFriese, Alice S. Hersh, and Margaret A. McManus, "A Proposed Research Agenda for Health Promotion and Disease Prevention for Children and the Elderly," *Health Services Research*, Part II, 19, no. 6 (n.d.): 1037.

10. Robert L. Kane, personal communication, December 1985.

11. Beth Soldo, chairman, Center for Population Research, Georgetown University, personal communication, December 1985.

12. Kane, personal communication, December 1985.

13. Ibid.

14. H. Maeda et al., "Nutritional Influences on Aging of Fischer 344 Rats: 2 Pathology," *Journal of Gerontology* 40 (1985): 671, as cited in Masoro, personal communication, 5 December 1985.

15. Masoro, personal communication, 5 December 1985.

16. Beth J. Soldo, Edmund D. Pellegrino, and James T. Howell, "Epilogue: Confronting the Age of Aging," *Socio-Economic Planning Science* 19, no. 4 (n.d.): 290.

17. Thomas Cole, assistant professor, Institute for the Medical Humanities, Medical Branch, University of Texas, Galveston, Tex., derived from personal communication, 12 December 1985.

18. Jordan Tobin, M.D., personal communication, 12 December 1985.

19. Charles Fahey, director, Third Age Center, Fordham University, personal communication, 23 November 1985.

20. Ibid.

21. Beth J. Soldo, personal communication, December 1985.

22. Cole, personal communication, 12 December 1985.

23. Jordan Tobin, M.D., personal communication, 12 December 1985.

24. Fernando Torres-Gil, staff director, House Select Committee on Aging, personal communication, 2 October 1985.

25. Robert L. Kane, personal communication, December 1985.

26. Robert L. Kane, derived from personal communication, December 1985.

27. M. Powell Lawton, personal communication, 21 November 1985.

28. Ibid.

29. Jordan Tobin, M.D., personal communication, 12 December 1985.

Appendix

Others who helped in the preparation of this report:

W. Andrew Achenbaum, Ph.D., Department of History, Carnegie-Mellon University, Pittsburgh, Pa.

George T. Baker III, Ph.D., Silver Spring, Md.

William Bechill, M.S.W., associate professor, School of Social Work and Community Planning, University of Maryland, Baltimore, Md.

William Birdsall, Ph.D., associate professor, School of Social Work, University of Michigan, Ann Arbor, Mich.

Elaine M. Brody, M.S.W., director, Department of Human Services, and senior researcher, Philadelphia Geriatric Center, Philadelphia, Pa.

Herman Brotman, consultant, Falls Church, Va.

Thomas Cole, assistant professor, Institute for the Medical Humanities, Medical Branch, University of Texas, Galveston, Tex.

Vincent J. Cristofalo, Ph.D., director, Center for the Study of Aging, University of Pennsylvania, Philadelphia, Pa.

William H. Crown, Ph.D., lecturer and senior research scholar, Florence Heller Graduate School, Brandeis University, Waltham, Mass.

Donald Fandetti, D.S.W., associate professor, School of Social Work and Community Planning, University of Maryland, Baltimore, Md.

Roger Feldman, Ph.D., professor, Department of Economics and School of Public Health, University of Minnesota, Minneapolis, Minn.

178

Frederick J. Ferris, D.S.W., administrator, AARP-Andrus Foundation, Washington, D.C.

Richard Getrost, beneficiary information specialist, Health Care Financing Administration, Washington, D.C.

Janet Giele, Ph.D., associate professor, Florence Heller Graduate School, Brandeis University, Waltham, Mass.

Robert Harootyan, analyst, Office of Technology Assessment, Washington, D.C.

Louis Harris and Associates, Inc., New York, N.Y.

Kalman Hettleman, J.D., associate professor, School of Social Work and Community Planning, University of Maryland, Baltimore, Md.

Karen Holden, Ph.D., Department of Economics, University of Wisconsin-Madison Campus, Madison, Wis.

Robert Hudson, Ph.D., professor, School of Social Work, Boston University, Boston, Mass.

Rosalie Kane, D.S.W., professor, School of Public Health, University of Minnesota, Minneapolis, Minn.

Library Staff, American Association of Retired Persons, Washington, D.C.

Phoebe S. Liebig, Ph.D., AARP Public Policy Institute, Washington, D.C.

Korbin Liu, Sc.D., senior research manager, National Center for Health Services Research, Rockville, Md.

Stephen R. McConnell, Ph.D., staff director, Senate Special Committee on Aging, Washington, D.C.

Edward Masoro, Ph.D., professor and chairman, Department of Physiology, University of Texas Health Science Center, San Antonio, Tex.

Harry R. Moody, Ph.D., deputy director, Brookdale Center on Aging, Hunter College, New York, N.Y.

Marilyn Moon, Ph.D., senior research associate, Urban Institute, Washington, D.C.

James N. Morgan, Ph.D., Institute for Social Research, University of Michigan, Ann Arbor, Mich.

Robert J. Myers, F.S.A., consulting actuary, Washington, D.C.

Bernice Neugarten, Ph.D., professor, Center for Public Policy, School of Education, Northwestern University, Evanston, Ill.

William Oriol, consultant, Silver Spring, Md.

Daniel Price, analyst, Office of Research, Statistics and International Policy, Social Security Administration, Washington, D.C.

Jon Pynoos, Ph.D., director, Program in Policy and Services Research, Andrus Gerontology Center, University of Southern California, Los Angeles, Calif.

Virginia Reno, director of the Program Analysis Staff, Office of Research, Statistics and International Policy, Social Security Administration, Washington, D.C.

Matilda W. Riley, D.Sc., associate director, Behavioral Sciences Research Program, National Institute on Aging, National Institutes of Health, Bethesda, Md.

Sara E. Rix, Ph.D., director, The Women's Research and Education Institute, Washington, D.C.

Phillip Rones, economist, Bureau of Labor Statistics, U.S. Department of Labor, Washington, D.C.

John Rother, director, Legislation, Research, and Public Policy Division, American Association of Retired Persons, Washington, D.C.

Bruce Schobel, F.S.A., actuary, Office of the Actuary, Social Security Administration, Washington, D.C.

Richard Schreitmueller, F.S.A., actuary, Office of the Actuary, Social Security Administration, Washington, D.C.

Harold Shepard, Ph.D., International Exchange Center on Gerontology, University of Southern Florida, Tampa, Fla.

Larry Smedley, Ph.D., associate director, Department of Occupational Safety, Health and Social Security, AFL-CIO, Washington, D.C.

Nancy H. Smith, M.A., professional staff, House Select Committee on Aging, Washington, D.C.

Paul Smith, Ph.D., director of research, Children's Defense Fund, Washington, D.C.

Henry Spiegelblatt, deputy director, Office of Intergovernmental Affairs, Health Care Financing Administration, Washington, D.C.

Constance Swank, Ph.D., special assistant to the director, Legislation, Research, and Public Policy Division, American Association of Retired Persons, Washington, D.C.

Cynthia Taeuber, M.A., special assistant for Selected Populations, Population Division, Bureau of the Census, Washington, D.C.

Cleonice Tavani, M.S.W., Department of Health and Human Services, Washington, D.C.

Jordan Tobin, M.D., chief, Human Performance Section, Gerontology Research Center, National Institute on Aging, National Institutes of Health, Baltimore, Md.

Fernando M. Torres-Gil, Ph.D., staff director, House Select Committee on Aging, Washington, D.C.

John Tropman, Ph.D., professor, School of Social Work, University of Michigan, Ann Arbor, Mich.

Jerry Turem, Ph.D., Washington, D.C.

Joan Van Nostrand, deputy director, Division of Health Care Statistics, National Center for Health Statistics, Department of Health and Human Services, Rockville, Md.

Elizabeth Vierck, M.M.H.S., private consultant, Washington, D.C.

Stanley Wenocur, D.S.W., associate professor, School of Social Work and Community Planning, University of Maryland, Baltimore, Md.

Index

Index

Aaron, Henry, 94-95
aging society:
    attitudes toward, 22, 23, 39, 137,
      174-175
    challenges facing, 21, 22, 39, 102,
      108
    characteristics of, 35-48
    costs incurred by, 21, 103, 141-142
    ethical issues confronting, 172-174
    implications of, 137-143
    opportunities presented by, 104-105
    significance of, 39
aged. *See* elderly
aged dependency ratio. *See* dependency
    ratio, aged
age group. *See* generation, defined
age sixty-five:
    increased longevity beyond, 63
    increased need for health care at,
      44-45, 50 n.20
    life expectancy at, 21, 37, 101-102,
      110
    Social Security benefits at, 92
Aid to Families with Dependent Children
    (AFDC), 121, 123, 146, 167
air pollution, 112
Alzheimer's disease, 60, 103-104, 143;
    see also chronic illness and disability
American Association of Retired Persons
    (AARP), 70, 95
American Council of Life Insurance, 71,
    152, 153
American Indians, 48, 120
Americans for Generational Equity
    (AGE), 147
arteriosclerosis, 44; *see also* chronic ill-
    ness and disability

arthritis, 44, 103; *see also* chronic illness
    and disability
asbestosis, 111
Asians and Pacific Islanders, 48
assets, as a source of income for elderly,
    41, 42, 86-89, 108, 109
Atlantic Monthly, 138

baby boom generation, 31, 117, 139, 147,
    170
    career-oriented women of, 65
    dearth of children among, 65-66
    growth of elderly population and, 21,
      35-37, 63
    retirement of, 21, 79n., 120, 129,
      138, 139, 169
    stake in future productivity of
      children, 119-120
Ball, Robert, 24-25, 80n.
Bane, Mary Jo, 144
biomedical research, 21, 170-171,
    173-174, 175-176
Binstock, Robert, 144, 151, 153
Birdsall, William, 82
birth, life expectancy at, 37
birth cohort. *See* generation, defined
birth weight, 111, 119
blacks:
    children, limited opportunities for,
      120
    health care for, limited, 111, 119
    health status among vs. whites, 47-48
    longevity among, 48
    mortality rates (life expectancy) of
      whites vs., 48, 111
    multigenerational households and,
      82-83

About the Authors

ERIC R. KINGSON joined the Graduate School of Social Work at Boston College in 1986 after seven years with the School of Social Work and Community Planning at the University of Maryland. His primary concern has been with Social Security, older worker and retirement issues, income maintenance policy, and services to the elderly. In 1982 he served as staff member of the National Commission on Social Security Reform, the bipartisan study group whose recommendations led to the amendments that resolved for the foreseeable future the financing problems of Social Security's cash programs. He hold a Ph.D. from Brandeis University's Florence Heller School, an M.P.A. from Northeastern University, and a B.A. from Boston University. He is the author of *Social Security and You*, a Ballantine paperback.

BARBARA A. HIRSHORN is a research fellow in the Population Studies Center at the University of Michigan, Ann Arbor. Her primary interests have been issues dealing with older workers, the productive use of time in old age, and forms of public and social support for older people. She has held a number of positions in research, planning, and policy analysis. She received a B.A. in sociology from the University of Wisconsin in 1969, an M.A. in communications from Syracuse University in 1977, and a Ph.D. in urban and regional planning from the University of Michigan in 1983.

JOHN M. CORNMAN has been executive director of The Gerontological Society of America since 1983. He was the chief executive officer of the National Rural Center from its founding in 1975 through its closing in 1982, an experience he drew on to write (with Barbara K. Kincaid) an instructive case history, *Lessons from Rural America*, which Seven Locks Press published as a book in 1984. Earlier, from 1969 to 1975, he was special assistant and director of communications for the late U.S. Senator Philip A. Hart. Before coming to Washington as a Congressional fellow in 1964, he was city editor of the *Daily Local News* in West Chester, Pennsylvania, for which he still writes a regular column on national affairs. A native of Philadelphia, he received his B.A. degree in English from Dartmouth College in 1955.